TURN ON YOUR LIFE

DR. MIKEL BROWN

Copyrighted Material

Turn On Your Life

Copyright © 2018 by Dr. Mikel Brown. All Rights Reserved.

No part of this publication may be reproduced, stored in a retrieval system or transmitted, in any form or by any means—electronic, mechanical, photocopying, recording or otherwise—without prior written permission from the publisher, except for the inclusion of brief quotations in a review.

Unless otherwise indicated, all Scripture quotation are taken from the New International Version of the Bible

For information about this title or to order other books and/or electronic media, contact the publisher:
CJC Publishing Company
1208 Sumac Drive, El Paso, Texas 79925
www.cjcpublishing.com

Library of Congress Control Number: 2017958115

ISBN: 978-1-930388-21-5 (Softcover)
        978-1-930388-22-2 (Hardcover)

Printed in the United States of America

Cover and Interior design: 1106 Design

Table of Contents

	Foreword	vii
	The Secret to Discovering Solutions	ix
1	Seven Ordinary Rules for Extraordinary Results	1
2	Take the Plunge	11
3	Get Motivated	17
4	Don't Just Sit There!	23
5	Avoid Verbal Contradictions	31
6	Back on Track	37
7	Become an Action Figure	43
8	Rethink Possible	55
9	Believe in Yourself	61
10	Choose All over Nothing at All	67
11	Contract and Build the Life and Business of Your Dreams	75
12	Devise Your Own Amazing Comeback	83
13	Disarming Pressure and Stress	91

14	Don't Suppress What You Possess	97
15	Don't Wait for the Chance of a Lifetime	107
16	Embrace Your Future	113
17	Explore Your Possibilities	123
18	Get the Gold	129
19	Get What Life Is Holding for You	135
20	Greatness Is a Decision Away	143
21	It Takes Everything to Win	147
22	Live Life Now!	151
23	Making Good Business Cents	155
24	Missing "U"	161
25	Need a Boost or a Boot?	167
26	Life's Purpose is Discovered While Helping Others Find Theirs	173
27	The Platinum Life Discovery	179
28	The Failures of the Successful	185
29	The Illusion of Greener Grass	193
30	The Strength of Perseverance	203
31	True Expectations	207
32	Upgrade Your Life (Style)	211
33	Wisdom for a Better Life	217
34	Uncompromised Dedication	225
	Index	231

DEDICATION

During my time on Earth, I have experienced many loves. I also learned how to love people in such a unique way which has opened up a bold new world of how love should be expressed without fear and vulnerability. This expression of love came from God not only for me to demonstrate to Him but to others as well. However, there is no person on earth I have grown to love and appreciate soooo much as my dear wife, Debra.

I now understand the movie *The Notebook* from an entirely different standpoint, and I'm glad I do. To my baby boy, Matthew, who showed up at the least expected time; you are your parents' revival of strength. To all my children and grandchildren whom I love and pray that God's blessings are lavishly appreciated.

It would be remiss of me to ignore the people who still believe in me after all these years—too many to name. Thank you—your support is deeply appreciated.

Foreword

In 2008, after a nine-year career, I retired from the National Basketball Association. Well, players like myself don't exactly retire. It's more like my services were no longer needed. Fortunately for me, I didn't have to look far for my next means of employment. The very day I got released, I was offered a coaching position with the Milwaukee Bucks'. Despite my longing to extend my playing career, I knew getting a coaching job at the professional level was an opportunity of a lifetime.

Nonetheless, like most retired players, I suffered quietly inside. After all, playing basketball had been a part of my life since the 7th grade. It was my identity. It was who I was. When I was forced to hang up my sneakers for good, I didn't know how to move past my playing days. It still pains me to say, but I was in a very lonely, dark place. Who am I? What is life about? How do I pick up the pieces and find the strength to move forward? My father, who was a pastor for 25 years, used to provide these answers for me, but a heart attack at the age of 47 sent him home to be with the Lord.

Desperately, I searched for answers, for meaning, but kept coming up short until one day, I went on LinkedIn. Yes, LinkedIn of all places! That's where I came across the profile of a man who had experience in working with elite professional athletes and personnel. My spirit was drawn to him. I didn't know who he was, but I knew God was telling me to reach out to him. And that's what I did. I contacted Dr. Brown out of the blue and told him that I needed his help. Even though he was a Laker fan, we hit it off immediately.

Today, I am so grateful to God that I took the bold step in contacting Dr. Brown because that one act of faith changed my life forever. Going into my 10th year of coaching, I can attest that I'm living my best life now, thanks to Dr. Brown. Be it family concerns or professional issues, I know I can always turn to Dr. Brown for the solution. I probably haven't done a good enough job of letting Dr. Brown know how much I have really appreciated his guidance and wisdom throughout the years.

There are not many African American men who are great models for us to follow. That is just a fact. But Dr. Brown is one of them. He is a pioneer, a counselor, and real professional in how he approaches any situation you bring to his attention. Therefore, I am confident that if you take a leap of faith like I did, and dive into *Turn on Your Life,* you will experience growth and happiness in your life like you have never experienced before.

There are answers out there for us. We don't have to go through life alone. Thankfully, we have people God uses to show us how we can make the best of our lives and that he loves and cares for us.

I appreciate Dr. Brown! Whenever he needs me, or when I just want to discuss my next move in life, I know that I have a consummate mentor in Dr. Brown!

Thank you, Dr. Brown, for letting God use you.

Adrian Griffin
Assistant Coach
Oklahoma City Thunder

The Secret to Discovering Solutions

"I believe that if you show people the problems and you show them the solutions they will be moved to act."
—Bill Gates

One of the reasons for people never finding the pie in the sky or living the American dream is because they have not discovered a problem to solve.

Building wealth is not a secret; it is having the insightful know-how to search for problems or inconveniences, and creating solutions for them. This is exactly what Madam C. J. Walker did to earn her millionaire status during a time when African Americans were considered subservient and uneducated people.

Madam C. J. Walker was born Sarah Breedlove on December 23, 1867, in Delta, Louisiana, to parents who were sharecroppers. She was one of six children and the first of her siblings born into freedom after the Emancipation Proclamation was signed. Her mother died, possibly from cholera, in 1872. Her father later remarried and died shortly afterward. With both of her parents dead, Sarah was left an orphan at the age of six.

Sarah moved in with her older sister and brother-in-law, Willie Powell. At the age of fourteen, she married Moses McWilliams, and three years later, her daughter, Lelia McWilliams, was born. When Sarah was twenty, her husband died, and shortly afterward she moved to St. Louis, where three of her brothers lived. They were all barbers at a local barbershop, and she managed to get a job as a washer woman. She barely earned more than a dollar a day but was determined to make enough money so that her daughter would be able to receive a formal education.

Many women of her era experienced hair loss primarily because of poor diet, hygiene practices and harsh products like lye that were included in soaps used to cleanse the hair. Most Americans lacked indoor plumbing, central heating and electricity; they bathed and washed their hair infrequently. Sarah initially learned about hair care from her brothers. Around the time of the 1904 World's Fair, she became a commission agent selling products for Annie Turnbo Malone, an African American hair-care entrepreneur.

While working on her hair care products in Denver, she married Charles Joseph Walker, a newspaper advertising salesman. It is said that she adapted her knowledge of hair and hair products while working with Annie Malone. During that time while working for Annie Malone she reemerged with the name Madam C. J. Walker, an independent hairdresser and retailer of cosmetic creams. She gave everyone the role model for a self-made businesswoman with her managerial skills and innovative marketing concepts. She began to organize her sales agents into local and state clubs. In 1917 she convened her first annual conference of the Madam

The Secret to Discovering Solutions

Walker Beauty Culturists in Philadelphia. She also started her own mail-order business to keep up with the booming business, placing her daughter A'Lelia Walker in charge of it.

Madam C. J. Walker developed a conditioning treatment for straightening hair. Starting with door-to-door sales of her cosmetics, Madam C. J. Walker amassed a fortune. In 1910 she built a factory in Indianapolis to manufacture her line of cosmetics. Before her death in 1919 she was a millionaire, one of the most successful business executives in the early half of the twentieth century. She was one of the first American women of any race or rank to become a millionaire through her own entrepreneurial efforts and solution-oriented business and sales models.

Are you overlooking the solution by only focusing on the problem? Understanding the origin of life's situations holds the key to discovering solutions to every problem.

The sphere of life is filled with the succession of time, energy, and quintessence of all material. Life is like one big space of nothing waiting to be developed. These spaces are our individual environments, which exist all around us, and we live our entire lives within this cavity called 'life.' The spaces which circumscribe our lives have within them the potential to produce whatever we decide to place within our personal vicinity. Inside this cavity holds everything life has to offer, and one can only access it if they have the ability to envision it and make it happen.

Problems and solutions are both neutral within our orb of existence and are only engendered when choices are made. However, if life seems to be problematic, then it must have had a creator to instigate its reality. The problem and the solution are one and the same because they are both created from the same substance. A problem originates as a result of the bad decisions or choices made which ignited the problem to materialize. Oftentimes, critical thinking must be applied in order to see the solution which hides in the crevasses of the problem.

> "Every problem has in it the seeds of its own solution. If you don't have any problems, you don't get any seeds."
> —Norman Vincent Peale

When an individual creates their own difficulty and tries to get others to repair it, it only exacerbates the problems. Solutions can be so easily discovered if a person would only go backward to the place before the problem began, to reconsider the choices which were made. Allowing others to come into the middle of your situation, to help bring a resolution to your concerns without understanding the origin of them, will be of no real significance to you. It's so much easier to suggest solutions when you don't know too much about the problem. Think about it, when the government tries to fix problems with private corporations, the government's solutions to their problems are usually as bad as the problems themselves; because the symptoms get the attention, not the problems.

True visionary people face the same problems everyone else faces. The only difference with the visionary is rather than becoming paralyzed by the problem, they immediately commit themselves to finding a solution by investigating the mechanics of that particular problem. Although some level of stress may exist within them, especially when there are time restraints to consider, they refuse to seek relief from the stress because they realize their focus will be misdirected away from finding the solution.

The Secret to Discovering Solutions

Let me quickly define the word 'problem,' because it may clear up some misconceptions you may have about a problem. A problem is something which is difficult to deal with, or it is difficulty understanding something or a source of trouble with the potential to result in anxiety. However, a 'solution' is defined as something used or done to deal with and end a problem, something which solves a problem or the condition of being solved.

Not everything or everyone you consider a problem actually exists as one. Some occurrences or people are only problems because this is the way a person may see them. A solution is like connecting the dots, which points to the answer. Some solutions may seem difficult, but not impossible to implement.

For instance, eating is not the problem for people who are overweight; however, what you eat and how much of it can be the problem to obesity. Changing what is eaten and how much is consumed is the solution to one's overweight condition. So, within the same context of eating as a problem, eating is also the solution—considering one governs their intake.

What if a person has money concerns? Like the problem with overindulgence of food, losing the excess weight is going to be a process. The only solution to money problems is money. The solution is not in having more money; the solution is in managing the money you have. You see, the solution is hidden in the problem itself. Finding a job paying twice the amount you are currently making will not answer your money concerns. When a person thinks this way, it is because they have no clue the extra money will only mask the problem and immediately deal with the symptom. But, when the extra money ointment wears off, they will be left with the same age-old problem.

There is no happiness in ignorance. Find your solutions before your problems start a serious revolution.

Turn on Your Life

> "Rarely do we find men who willingly engage in hard, solid thinking. There is an almost universal quest for easy answers and half-baked solutions. Nothing pains some people more than having to think."
> —Martin Luther King, Jr.

CHAPTER ONE

Seven Ordinary Rules for Extraordinary Results

"Insanity: doing the same thing over and over again and expecting different results."
—Albert Einstein

Growth won't come from what you already know—it will come from receiving information that you didn't know.

When he was seventeen, Charles Dutton, of the sitcom *Roc*, got into a fight that resulted in a man's death. Dutton was convicted of manslaughter, and he spent the next two years in prison. Several months after being released, Dutton was arrested for possession of a deadly weapon and was sentenced to three years in prison.

During his second prison term, Dutton was sentenced to six days of solitary confinement, and only allowed to take one book with him. By chance, he grabbed a book called *The Anthology of Black Playwrights*. He enjoyed the plays so much that, upon his release from confinement, he petitioned the warden to start a drama group for the Christmas talent show. After his release from prison, Dutton earned a master's degree in acting from the Yale School of Drama and went on to pursue his love of acting on both TV and the big screen.

What's the secret of the people who seem to get such incredible results despite the fact that they are working with basically the same pool of resources as you are? No one person has any special "achievability" power that other people don't have. Everyone has made unbelievable mistakes, and yet, some have had breakdowns while others have had breakthroughs. It comes down to how proficient people are in the use of their abilities.

Are you aware of the paralyzing effects of fear? How it strangles your thinking and immobilizes you from taking action? In fact, fear is responsible for engendering indecisiveness that results in failed attempts to make necessary changes to better your life. Some of the most talented people who lack self-confidence will procrastinate in making a decision rather than risk failure, and every lost opportunity erodes a person's confidence, leading to a downward spiral.

Each year around March, people start giving up on their goals for the New Year. Believe it or not, most people forget what they committed to for the year anyway. I'm amazed at how each year slips by just a little more quickly. Yet most people don't bat an eye at the amount of time they waste procrastinating and contemplating. How can people so easily give up on their New Year hopes so early in the game? A "new year" is not sixty days into the next year—it is 365 days! You have time to make it a great New Year.

If you are not experiencing success or freedom, and you find yourself in the same or a worse position than the previous year, you are either missing knowledge or not properly executing and maximizing the knowledge you possess. Viktor Frankl explained it like this: "Life is never made unbearable by circumstances, but only by lack of meaning and purpose."

Allow me to give you seven ordinary rules that you can apply to your life to produce seven extraordinary results. When you apply these seven rules, your mind will burst into a thousand suns and you will never see your life the same again.

1. KNOW THE POWER OF THE PRESENT

All you are guaranteed is now. God may hold the future in His hands, but you control the content of what happens for you. If you are not taking action now on what you say is important and meaningful, you are designing a life that guarantees what you say is important will never occur. The Bible says in 2 Corinthians 6:2 "now [is] the accepted time." It is unrealistic to think that you can stretch now into someday. Someday is not a day of the week.

NOW is the acronym for No Opportunities Wasted! You have to seize the present moment and make things happen. You are your greatest asset, not your worst nightmare. Don't be afraid to explore you. You have incredible talents and gifts waiting to be discovered. Go ahead, unwrap yourself. You will be astonished by the things you can do that you once considered impossible.

Make up in your mind that you are not going to allow your NOW moment to pass you by. When it comes time to shine, overcome your shyness or fear and don't allow these things to rob you of your moment. Turn your life light on and let people know that you are here to stay. Brighten up your workplace, your home, and your business. Own your power moment.

Every morning as you open your eyes, be ready to experience a day that you have never seen before. God is actually opening the curtain of life for your NOW moment! Imagine hearing the announcer echoing these words to the entire universe: "All of creation, this day, I present to you the greatest of God's creation, (your name). Stand and applaud, as (your name) performs the incredible feats of delving into his or her ability to change the world."

Wow! Wow! Wow! I bet you never imagined this could be possible, but it is. Can you hear the applause from the trees, the flowers, the sun and moon, the clouds, the earth, and all that are in it? They are all waiting for you to perform the "I cans" and "I wills" of the day. And, at the close of the day, take a bow as the earth gives you a standing ovation. Then when you have shut your eyelids for the night, the curtain closes, waiting for tomorrow to present you with a new now moment—your power moment.

Don't frivolously spend your time on "I can'ts." You will never get anything of significance done.

2. Choose a Powerful Attitude

An attitude is a settled way of thinking or feeling, typically reflected in a person's behavior. Consistently checking your attitude is one of the keys to maximizing yourself. Your attitude will determine your altitude of accomplishments or the depth of your despair. In the words of Winston Churchill, "Attitude is a little thing that makes a big difference." Don't ever underestimate the power of your attitude, because your attitude gives birth to your actions. All actions are thoughts and emotions manifested. You are accountable for your own attitude and the direction it takes you.

You can be all dressed up on the outside going to a job interview, but inwardly, you are wearing old coveralls and feeling bruised, defeated, and hopeless about your future. What do you think you will convey through your personality when you have constant thoughts of defeat? Viktor Frankl said, "When we are no longer able to change a situation, we are challenged to change ourselves"—that is, to change our attitudes.

Attitudes drive behavior. Your body language is a result of your attitude. Your attitude sends out a message that everyone consciously or unconsciously understands. It is imperative that you learn and master potent personal strategies to keep yourself thinking and acting positive and creatively. Just because you didn't like a decision your boss made doesn't mean you have to show it. The lack of enthusiasm or confidence displayed in your attitude will certainly keep you on the low end of the pay scale.

3. Take Responsibility for Your Perceptions

How you perceive people and events ultimately determines your attitude toward them and how you will react to them as they occur. It is commonly noted that perception equals reality. Therefore, you can easily change your reality by changing your perception of any situation. By regularly opening yourself to new information, you will be able to change your perceptions, thereby altering your reality.

Reality changes as you open your heart and mind to up-to-the-minute information. I have been in the business of counseling people for over thirty years, and what I see and hear is that no one likes to mentally be in a bad place, feeling like there is no way of escape. Everyone wants to change what they do not like about their life, career, or marriage, but many of these people do not have the solution on how to generate the permanent change they so desire.

If there was any one person who knew how to change his reality, it was Paul of Tarsus in the Bible. But first allow me to inform you that every point I'm making in parentheses about this scripture from the Bible is my personal explanation. In Philippians 3:13, Paul said "but this is one thing [I do], forgetting (*dismember*) those things which are behind (*so that they become unrecognizable*), (*which will cause me to overlook or lose from the mind*) and reaching forth unto those things which are before." You cannot reach for your future while your hands are behind your back reaching to your past.

Stop going to the people from your past and searching for affirmation from them. Many of your friends and respected colleagues are still living in what "used to be" while you are escaping to what "ought to be." Find someone who is winning in areas where you are losing, and you will find someone who is living in a different reality than you are. What do they see that you are blind to? What do they know that you are missing? Move closer to them, because only then can you see and experience what they see and live on a daily basis.

4. Be Conscientious About Your Impact

If you wish to create a new result, you must first take a new action. I have personally learned that you cannot complain about what you tolerate. If you don't like your results in a given area of your work or life, pay careful attention to what you are now doing. Whatever you do habitually, they are the occurrences you rehearsed in your mind. Aristotle said, "We are what we repeatedly do. Excellence, then, is not an act, but a habit." What happens in life is not an accident but a result of consistent actions.

Not only do your actions affect your life, but they also affect the lives of your distant admirers. People can appear to have all the success and "toys" of life, but in reality they are suffocating themselves with debt. When others look on and see what apparently represents success, they will try to emulate it and fall into the same trap.

Watch your words and your actions; your future is hoping that you don't repeat your past.

5. COMMIT TO SELF-DEVELOPMENT, NOT SELF-DESTRUCTION

I strongly encourage people to consider doing things for themselves before working to improve the lives of others. If you correct yourself before you correct others, if you love yourself before you love others, and if you become your own friend before you try becoming a friend of others, you will better understand how to help others. This should not be considered selfishness, but self-development. Once you balance the world inside you, you can then help others to balance their worlds.

If you do things only for pleasure, you are actually missing the point of life, which involves the lives of others. No man is an island. When you become a success, it will help others to become successes as well. If you are not responsible, you will spend your days trying to either feel good or avoid feeling bad. The best way to fulfill life is to help others succeed after you have helped yourself to succeed.

If you are that person who is always trying to offer advice in areas where you do not have a history of success, you may be the kind of person who seeks to control people and their environments. This control is an illusion because there is no freedom in it. Don't pretend to be what you are not in order to project the image that you know more than what you actually know. There is a higher purpose and drive that should encompass your heart and mind.

The highest state of existence is to offer yourself in sacrifice to serve God, others, or a cause. Understanding your life's purpose will inspire you to move forward.

When you know your personal values and discover your life's purpose, you are on your way to achieving your life goals. You will have more time to assist others in discovering their purposes while achieving work and life balance for yourself. With a balanced life, you will be less stressed, and you will make decisions with clarity and focus.

Your self-esteem (the opinion you have of yourself) is closely related to how intimate you are with your life's purpose. The more you know what you love to do, the more you are in tune with yourself, the more fulfilled you feel, and the higher your self-esteem will be. Not knowing your purpose and, at the same time, refusing to pursue it will eventually lead to self-destruction. In the words of Kofi Annan, "To live is to choose. But to choose, you must know who you are and what you stand for, where you want to go, and why you want to get there."

6. ACT IN ACCORDANCE WITH YOUR BELIEFS

Your strong beliefs will birth powerful actions. Selling out on your belief system is the equivalent of amputating your own limbs. There is no power in pretense or compromise. When you attend church on Sunday, singing hymns on helping your fellow man, and yet pursue power and pleasure on Monday, making decisions that hurt and wound others, you are being a house divided against itself: you will not succeed, and you will not stand.

You don't always act according to your conscious thoughts and spoken utterances. The reason for this is that unconscious forces drive your behavior. These include your habits of thinking patterns that come from putting life on automatic, which ultimately disconnects your actions from what you really want. Therefore, parts of your life are out of sync with each other. Think of a man who wears a safety helmet when cycling, then stops and has a cigarette; or a mother who tells her children not to waste food because of the millions who are starving, yet who has a closet full of clothes she's hardly ever worn.

You may want to succeed financially, but you are doing everything to suggest that right now is not the time to reach your financial aspirations. You want more money, but you stay away from financial seminars on how to get it. You may be more divided than you would ever like to admit. You are wired for success but programmed for failure. If you can accept this present reality, you will be on your way to aligning yourself with what you believe.

Discover what your true beliefs are, and if they are favorable, stick to them. If they are not what you personally desire, change them and then stick to the new ones. Be a person of conviction, not preference. People of preference have nothing to stand on because their foundations are like shifting sand. They are always reevaluating what is important to them based on what is important to others. However, people of conviction know what and in whom they have believed and care nothing about how others may feel about it. This is what drives them to succeed and reach maximum results.

7. Keep in Mind that Anything Is Possible

You may decide what is possible for your life by looking at your past and predicting the future. This is designing your future from your past, usually by repeating a slightly different version of it. Imagine a place where all your opportunities are locked away in one place. You own the key, but you cannot find it. If a question like this seems to intrigue you, imagine the feeling of knowing that you have millions of dollars, but you cannot get access to it.

You don't just want what is locked away behind the invisible door of impossibilities, but you need what has been stored away for you for so long. Nevertheless, you have become so accustomed to living without it that the thought of getting your hands on it seems elusive. Until now—the key to unlock all your possibilities is about to be discovered.

THE KEY

It all started for me in the early nineties when I became convinced that what I needed, I already had. Have you ever looked for your glasses only to discover that they were on you the whole time? I had to learn the hard-hitting, honest-to-goodness truth that if my problem was my creation, then so was my solution. I could custom build and meticulously handcraft a life that is built to last.

Anything unrecognized becomes uncelebrated and unrewarded. Recognizing your potential can be the difference of a lifetime of success or failure. Your income can change, your marriage can change, your weight can change, and your life can change—all for the better. Change is really an effortless accomplishment.

Now that you have accepted the reality of what can change, change "can" to "will" and watch what happens over time. Go ahead; you have the right to exercise the audacity to say whatever you want to change. You can, and you will!

When you feel out of balance, refer back to these seven ordinary rules and identify which rule you have not taken as your reality. Immediately apply that rule, and you will restore your life's balance. And remember—if you don't manage your life according to your values, life will manage you according to your emotions.

CHAPTER TWO
Take the Plunge

"When you have confidence, you can have a lot of fun.
And when you have fun, you can do amazing things."
—Joe Namath

The picture you have of yourself is so important that, if your mental picture is distorted, so will be your life. You will never feel that your life has much value because you will always feel less fortunate than everyone else.

There once lived a very wealthy man who was renowned for his great wealth and his liberality. Certain friends of younger days came to him and said: "You are more fortunate than we. You have become very rich while we struggle with simply existing. You can wear the finest garments and you can enjoy the rarest foods, while we must be content if we can dress our families in clothes that are presentable and feed them as best we can. Once we were equal. We studied under the same instructors. We played in the same games. And in neither the studies nor the games did you outshine us. And in the years since, you have been no more honorable a citizen than we. Nor have you worked harder or more faithfully, insofar as we can judge. Why then should a fickle fate single you out to enjoy all the good things of life and ignore us, who are equally deserving?"

The wealthy man said to them, "If you have not acquired more than a bare existence in the years since we were youths, it is because you either have failed to learn the laws that govern the building of wealth, or else you do not observe them."

When I read this story for the first time, I realized why most people choose to believe that if someone is wealthy, then it must be an act of fate—that destiny has everything to do with someone being successful and wealthy, and nothing else. This would cause the average person to believe that wealth only comes by chance and not by deliberate means. This, however, I cannot believe nor accept as reality. The truth of the matter is that wealth building is more of a methodical and intentional act than an unintentional one. The only people who are millionaires without having built their wealth over time are people who have won the lottery—and money gained quickly is often gone just as fast.

The friends of the wealthy man from the story may have grown up with him, but their realities were not the same. People can have all the talent in the world, but if they don't know what to do with that talent, all they have is information without transformation. Information is supposed to open people's eyes and broaden their horizons. Instead, when information is not converted into adhered knowledge and then that knowledge into energy, a person is left with knowledge but no experience.

Is your potential locked away inside of a safe to which you have forgotten the combination? Do you feel at times you have so much stored away inside without any way of letting it out? You're gifted, talented, and smart, but you don't have a clue how to unlock your specific gifts that can help you consistently reach your goals and mushroom your peak performance. This is something you have been searching for all your life, and you feel like discovering it is right around the corner. You know you want more, you need more, and there is more. And you want to develop your potential so that you can increase your chances of a more personally productive life, increase your income, improve your lifestyle, and experience a wonderful relationship with your significant other.

You are on the hunt, tracking your purpose. You are a searcher. You want a richer life, a fuller life. You hate the feeling of being bottled up or stored away like old news. Your challenges are not tougher than you are, but your lack of knowledge in certain matters exposes the cracks in your defenses, and you end up repeating many of the same struggles. The power of release can easily be turned into the release of power or potential.

You can reach your goals, achieve the unthinkable, and experience success in every single area of your life. However, it is not going to happen when you choose to settle for what you did not aim for. When you are operating at your peak performance levels, you feel extraordinarily incredible and nothing can stand in the way of you achieving your goals, which is the quintessential of living your dreams. You will feel like you're on top of the world. This is what you want! Believe me—this is what you need!

Principles (laws that govern practices) need to be intimately understood before you can think of being practical or efficient. At the same time, you acquire experience through action, rather than through theory, speculation, or ideals. For example: A person gains practical experience in the game of basketball by first learning the rules and then playing the game. Imagine if Michael Jordan did not understand the rules of the game. All his potential would have meant absolutely nothing. The referees would have made all kinds of calls against him because he would have constantly violated the laws of the game. Understand the significance of principles and the importance of putting them into practice, and the sky will be the limit.

THE POWER TO DECIDE

Whatever is lost or ruined by ignorance or devastation can be restored through a simple release of your personal power to decide. It is your nature to seek more because you desire more. I have never met a person who did not expect to inhale his or her next breath after exhaling the carbon dioxide.

People's images of themselves are often self-defeating. They look at and size themselves up by weight, height, body type (fat, skinny, short, or tall), and ability, and deem themselves less than others. When you compare, you will compete, and it is not fair to compete against others when they are unaware they are in a competition.

The world was shocked when a video went viral on the Internet a few years ago of a virtually unknown singer named Susan Boyle, who tried out for a TV talent show in Great Britain. She was a little on the heavy side and middle-aged, and it was quite obvious that the judges and the audience did not take her seriously when she first walked onto the stage. But then she began to sing . . . everyone in the audience, including the biggest critic of them all, Simon Cowell, was enthralled by her voice. I truly believe that those who saw and heard Susan Boyle sing learned a lifelong lesson—people should not judge a book by its cover. Susan Boyle took the plunge, figuring, "What do I have to lose?" She may have initially received laughs and subtle smiles when she walked out on that stage, but after she finished, her audience was in tears and gave her a standing ovation.

Susan knew her talent and what she was capable of doing with it. However, her audience was not aware of it. She knew that she could sing, but she was also aware that her physical appearance may have made her voice not enough in the eyes of the professionals. When Simon asked her age, she said that she was forty-seven, with her hand on her hip, as if to say, "What does age have to do with what I came to do?"

Today, Susan Boyle sings on world stages, not just in her shower. What about you? Are you going to say, "Forget my fear . . . I'm going for it!" Or are you going to sit around for the rest of your life and watch other people, less talented and less committed, do what you know you can do to perfection?

Talented people know what tools they possess. They also know how to stretch their talent and do amazing things with it because they do them often in private. The problem is that many of these talented people do not believe in themselves. They are mentally challenged by their own self-induced apprehensions. When the picture they have of themselves changes, then every facet of their lives is going to change. However, people who assume that they are talented and gifted must not take a presumptuous dive into a fantasy of wishes without the full belief that what they are doing has nothing to do with presumption.

The encouragement and tutelage of others have their place, but you have to believe so deeply in what you are capable of doing that you don't care what people think of you. You are ready to show the world what you have. Don't look for applause before you show your stuff. Believe me, applause will come later, after your performance; just get out there and do your thing. James Cameron put it, "If you wait until the right time to have a child you'll die childless, and I think filmmaking is very much the same thing. You just have to take the plunge and just start shooting something even if it's bad."

What Does It Mean to Take the Plunge?

Taking the plunge is doing something important or difficult that you have been thinking about doing or waiting a lifetime to get the guts to do. It means diving in and going all the way. The odds of success are considerably higher if you put the same level of effort, enthusiasm, and commitment into what you do on the job that you do into what you do off it. In fact, you will have a legitimate shot at success.

You may have played it safe all of your life. Don't you think it's time to stop playing games with your life? You still have the rest of your life remaining. Choose not to live inundated with regrets. You only have one life to live; live it until no more life in you remains. Own your own ladder and climb it to the top.

CHAPTER THREE

Get Motivated

"To succeed, you need to find something to hold on to, something to motivate you, something to inspire you."
—Tony Dorsett

The person who is hungry for something will eat; and the one who wants to achieve success in life, business, or sports, will motivate him or herself from within—for that is all the motivation needed.

In 1883, a creative engineer named John Roebling was inspired by an idea to build a spectacular bridge connecting New York with Long Island. However, bridge building experts throughout the world thought that this was an impossible feat and told Roebling to forget the idea. It just could not be done. It was not practical. It had never been done before.

Roebling could not ignore the vision he had in his mind of this bridge. He thought about it all the time and knew deep in his heart that it could be done. He just had to share the dream with someone else. After much discussion and persuasion he managed to convince his son Washington, an up-and-coming engineer, that the bridge in fact could be built.

Working together for the first time, the father and son developed concepts of how it could be accomplished and how the obstacles could be overcome. With great excitement and inspiration, and the headiness of a wild challenge before them, they hired their crew and began to build their dream bridge.

The project started well, but when it was only a few months underway a tragic accident on the site took the life of John Roebling. Washington was also injured and left with a certain amount of brain damage, which resulted in him not being able to talk or walk.

"We told them so."

"Crazy men and their crazy dreams."

"It's foolish to chase wild visions."

Everyone had a negative comment to make and felt that the project should be scrapped since the Roeblings were the only ones who knew how the bridge could be built.

In spite of his handicap, Washington was never discouraged and still had a burning desire to complete the bridge, and his mind was still as sharp as ever. He tried to inspire and pass on his enthusiasm to some of his friends, but they were too daunted by the task.

As he lay on his bed in his hospital room with the sunlight streaming through the windows, a gentle breeze blew the flimsy white curtains apart, and he was able to see the sky and the tops of the trees outside for just a moment.

It seemed that there was a message for him not to give up. Suddenly an idea hit him. All he could do was move one finger, and he decided to make the best use of it. By moving this, he slowly developed a code of communication with his wife.

He touched his wife's arm with that finger, indicating to her that he wanted her to call the engineers again. Then he used the same method of tapping her arm to tell the engineers what to do. It seemed foolish, but the project was under way again.

For thirteen years Washington tapped out his instructions with his finger on his wife's arm, until the bridge was finally completed. Today the spectacular Brooklyn Bridge stands in all its glory as a tribute to the triumph of one man's indomitable spirit and his determination not to be defeated by circumstances. It is also a tribute to the engineers and their teamwork, and to their faith in a man who was considered mad by half the world. It stands, too, as a tangible monument to the love and devotion of his wife, who for thirteen long years patiently decoded the messages of her husband and told the engineers what to do.

Perhaps this is one of the best examples of a never-say-die attitude that overcomes a terrible physical handicap and achieves an impossible goal.

Often when we face obstacles in our day-to-day life, our hurdles seem very small in comparison to what many others have to face. The Brooklyn Bridge shows us that dreams that seem impossible can be realized with determination and persistence, no matter what the odds are.

When you know someone else has done what you are endeavoring to accomplish, then you know you can do it, too. It's easy to see someone else do something and then believe you can do it. But what happens when there is no record of anyone ever accomplishing or even attempting what your dream has inspired you to do? Steve Jobs once said, "Your time is limited, so don't waste it living someone else's life. Don't be trapped by dogma—which is living with the results of other people's thinking. Don't let the noise of others' opinions drown out your own inner voice. And most important, have the courage to follow your heart and intuition."

Do you have that feeling deep in your gut that it's time to go for it, to tackle the one thing you've waited your whole life to make happen? You realize you can no longer fight that feeling, that thought—when you feel you are against the odds, even though someone else has already done what you aspire to accomplish, and you have that belief, that drive and determination that you can do it, too. This crazy feeling swimming around inside your gut is the audacity that will keep you strong and persistent, always challenging yourself to do it. When you have a real-to-life dream, it becomes necessary that you live this dream.

There is talk about how people are slowly dying because of what they eat. I say that might be true; however, many people are dying from what's eating them. When you know that you can do more than what you're doing—have more than what you have—life will eat you up with regrets if you don't put all your effort into making it happen. It will slowly eat away at your self-confidence, your inner belief; you will regret not ever having lived your dream. You will feel a hurt inside that you cannot explain. You will not be able to pinpoint where it hurts; you will just know it hurts. It is a pain that literally pokes you from the inside because you know in your heart of hearts that life holds more for you than what you are presently experiencing.

Understand this: when you are seeking what your purpose is and you are feverishly working to make life work for you, instead of you working hard to make a life, life takes on a new sense of adventure. It is mentally healthy to have a dream to pursue because it keeps your mind engaged. When you decide to settle to be less than what you are, to enjoy less than what you are capable of producing, and to sit in the comfort chair of mediocrity, you will begin a slow descent into your demise.

People with dreams live longer lives than people without them. When you have a dream to live, you are better off than the person who has to live with no dream at all. You will have a different kind of energy about you. Not only are you extending your life, but you are adding life to your years, making it more enjoyable. This is when you understand that your dream is not optional—it's necessary. You have this acute awareness that if you don't do something about your dream, it's going to eat at you and drive you crazy.

You have got to find your thing! Whatever it is, it is necessary that you do it. Until you own your dream, it will remain a fantasy. Stop walking around with a long face and a short pocketbook. The moment you realize that your dream is not optional, but that it is necessary, you will discover your own life force. In fact, the prison that held you back was not a prison at all, but rather a figment of your imagination.

GET MOTIVATED! STAY MOTIVATED!

CHAPTER FOUR

Don't Just Sit There!

"My attitude is that if you push me towards something that you think is a weakness, then I will turn that perceived weakness into a strength."
—Michael Jordan

*To make a decision generates movement;
to make no decision keeps you static.*

ONE DAY, a young protégé of mine was concerned with a particular problem and sought my thoughts on his situation. He told me that his problem needed immediate attention. He said that if he did not make a decision about the matter today, it could cost him a considerable amount of money. After he informed me of his circumstances, I addressed his issue. My recommendation to him was to call the company first thing in the morning about his concession and send an e-mail detailing his reasons. After several days had passed, I happened to see him, and I inquired about his decision concerning his problem. He said that he and his wife had decided to hold off on making any decision and that they would call the company next week. I asked, "Do you think that your problem is going to go away?"

He replied, "These things have a funny way of working themselves out."

My response was utter silence, and I concluded the conversation with, "Good day."

How can people be so naïve as to think that if things were left to themselves they would evolve into something beautiful? That makes as much sense as does believing that the destroyed Twin Towers in New York could evolve into two new towers all on their own. Unless there is human involvement in cleaning up and starting over again, the debris of the explosion would remain.

Do you believe in chance? Do you leave your problems alone, thinking that somehow they will work themselves out? Do you leave your life to a belief in luck? It may be time to reconsider. Lucille Ball once said, "Luck? I don't know anything about luck. I've never banked on it, and I'm afraid of people who do. Luck to me is something else: hard work and realizing what is opportunity and what isn't." Success yields itself to self-disciplined and driven individuals who believe that they can force their success.

No marriage works without sacrifices, no business succeeds without a proven product or service, and no person overcomes ignorance without information and applied knowledge. You must make something happen. I have trained many people to succeed in life and business; however, the most difficult people to train are the ones who trained themselves not to listen.

Decisions are at the heart of success, and there are critical moments when they can be difficult, perplexing, and even nerve-racking. Every successful person has had help and guidance for making efficient and effective decisions. To put it another way, the vision for your business and future is often impinged on by what you believe about the world you live in. Your beliefs often determine the information that you can easily distinguish because it is formed to bear a resemblance to what you trust the most.

So, decision making is about facing a question, such as "To be or not to be?" That is a question that only a decision can make clear. Humanity has always lived in the shadow of fears and uncertainties. These fears often keep us in limbo until they are eradicated so that the consequences of our choices can be properly weighed without the apprehension of failure. This fear of making the wrong decisions should be well-known to any responsible manager. Eleanor Roosevelt said, "You gain strength, courage, and confidence by every experience in which you really stop to look fear in the face." You can be assured that wherever you see successful millionaire and billionaire business owners, these are people who are familiar with making courageous decisions. They realize, and many of them have learned from experience, that it can be quite costly to delay a decision. There has never yet been a person in humanity's history who led a life of ease, whose name is worth remembering for achieving anything worthwhile.

Forethought Is Time Travel

Much of our lives is uncharted territory because we live them one moment at a time. If you want to change your financial condition or sculpt your dream into a business and money-making machine, you must decide to live with intent. Having foresight is anticipating your next move and seeing the possible challenges and snares that might lie ahead. This will help you avoid being derailed on your journey to success.

Experiencing success by accident is like winning a lottery. You might have won millions, but because of your lack of experience with handling millions of dollars, you have a 73 percent chance of shrinking back to the income level you were on before you won the lottery.

If there is anything that will expose you to solutions during a crisis, it is the realization that crises are normal to life. How you see a crisis will be quintessential to how you deal with it. When you see crises as only misfortunes, they conceal the opportunities that are just underneath. The word "crisis" is from the Greek, meaning "a moment to decide." The chronic recurrent moments of crisis and decision, when understood, are growth junctures, points of initiation that denote release from one state of being and growth into the next.

When I hear somebody sigh, "Life is hard," I am always tempted to ask, "Compared to what?" When life is hard, you constantly have to react to situations that occurred because you did not act when the opportunity was presented. A life of reaction is a life of slavery—intellectually and spiritually. One must fight for a life of action, not reaction.

When you're faced with unfamiliar conditions or a situation that demands an immediate response and answers are not readily available, what will be your primary source of information? It is situations like these that test your resolve and gauge your ability to apply critical thinking. It's not stress that kills us; it is our reaction to it. Knowing what you want and making decisions based on you getting it puts you on the right track. However, being on the right track is not enough to ensure that you are going to make it. Even if you are on the right track, you will get run over if you just sit there. Taking action may not always be what you want to do; but without it, there will be no results. Ideas without actions are worthless! Start by doing what is necessary, then do what's possible, and suddenly you are doing the impossible.

Why do we need to read books about money, business, motivation, and inspiration when we want to be successful? Why do you need to breathe is my answer? Reading the book of a respected, wealthy, business person is the most inexpensive way of employing the services of a business coach. You need the association of those who represent who you are, what you are made of, and where you are going to become all you are supposed to be. People help to heal people, and people help people to grow.

A wise man once articulated an idea recorded in the Bible, Proverbs 27:17: "As iron sharpens iron, so one man sharpens another." When you develop camaraderie with people of like passions, their hindsight can become your foresight.

One of the reasons I like pouring my wisdom and knowledge into people who appreciate and respect my advice is because they put the information to use. There is nothing that says celebration to a teacher or coach like someone who appropriates advice by putting it to use in their own lives. However, those who make no investment into their lives after buying my books or purchasing quality motivational and instructional CDs that can help frame their thinking patterns speak volumes about what they think of me. Advice is seldom welcome; and those who need it the most always like it the least.

I can see where a person is going in life by watching their habits and their associations. People who consider themselves victims of their circumstances will always remain victims unless they develop greater vision for their lives. People who are confused are usually that way because they have a difficult time separating between the voices that are important and the ones that are not. Seeking information from one hundred people will get you one hundred different answers. This is why constructive criticism should never be solicited from critical people.

You have to be careful with whom you connect, because you are sharing influences. If their influence is greater than yours and they are unbalanced in their personal view of life and business, you may find yourself more governed by their influence than by their advice. My advice would be to run as far as you can away from these people. You will eventually find yourself more confused than you were when you first entered their presence.

Where does indecisiveness come from? Knowing the answer to this question will help you discover the key to being decisive and strong-minded. In order to succeed in life or business, and to make a lot of money, you have to apply clear-thinking approaches to your goals.

Indecisiveness is birthed out of too many options. For example, restaurants with extensive menus find that people with too many options usually take longer to serve and are constantly changing their order. This creates a bottleneck in the kitchen area and dissatisfied customers overall. However, menus that make it easier to order and that are seldom changed result in customers being served much faster, thus creating happy customers and an easier flow in the kitchen.

Don't make your life complex. Simplify your life by narrowing down your choices and knowing what it is you want. You will be surprised that the majority of the American public is either too afraid to mention what they really want in life for fear of what others may say or they do not know what they want. Many only know that they don't want to continue living in the state they are living now.

Life really holds simple answers for what people usually call complex problems. Just make a decision by cutting all the former hindrances away and tie yourself to your future. Remember to tie a rope of your dreams around your waist and tie it tight, because when your hands get tired of holding on, the rope of your dreams will still be around your waist so that it holds on to you.

Make your decision now! Don't just sit there with that woe-is-me look on your face. Do something, and do it NOW! Whatever you decide to do when you get up, decide you will accomplish exactly what you got up to do.

CHAPTER FIVE

AVOID VERBAL CONTRADICTIONS

"He that would live in peace and at ease must
not speak all he knows or all he sees."
—BENJAMIN FRANKLIN

*You cannot reason with failure, nor can you change
the minds of people, but you can change yourself.
You are always in charge of yourself.*

As a drought continued for what seemed an eternity, a small community of farmers was in a quandary as to what to do. Rain was important to keep their crops healthy and sustain the way of life of the townspeople.

The problem became more acute, and a local pastor called a prayer meeting to ask for rain. Many people arrived. The pastor greeted most of them as they filed in. As he walked to the front of the church to officially begin the meeting, he noticed most people were chatting across the aisles and socializing with friends. When he reached the front, his thoughts were on quieting the attendees and starting the meeting.

His eyes scanned the crowd as he asked for quiet. He noticed an eleven-year-old girl sitting quietly in the front row. Her face was beaming with excitement. Next to her, ready for use, was a bright red umbrella. The little girl's beauty and innocence made the pastor smile as he realized how much faith she possessed. No one else in the congregation had brought an umbrella. All came to pray for rain—a verbal commitment—but the little girl had come expecting God to answer—planned action in the form of a bright red umbrella.

People who recognize me when I'm out and about usually like to stop me to ask a question or two about a concern of theirs. Typically the first thing to come out of their mouths is a brief résumé on who they are and what they've done. Well, one young man was telling me about how he was going to start eating right and taking care of his body. He spoke about vegetables and the benefits of eating them on a daily basis. He admitted, "I'm killing myself with my bad eating habits," and followed it immediately by saying, "I have to go outside and have a cigarette."

I was not shocked by his statement. People often speak contradictorily. Their actions affirm the opposite of their words. My wife often says, "People just like to hear themselves speak, even if they know they aren't saying anything important."

Committing to do something and actually doing it is very difficult. People often give themselves leniency when it comes to their mediocre attempts to follow through on what they say. They don't acknowledge the truth that they really do not believe they are capable of doing what they say. Some people say they want to be rich, but

Avoid Verbal Contradictions

they work a nine-to-five job. This is a contradiction of terms. I have never seen anyone, nor heard of anyone, ever getting rich working a job. Others claim they are working hard to lose weight, but they go on subsequent fast-food binges. It seems to me that the only thing these people are working hard at is finding the nearest burger joint.

Some people claim they want success, but they are afraid of failure. People want to be happy and live a life of significance, but they avoid vulnerable relationships where they may be emotionally hurt. These people have never heard or do not believe that the deeper sorrow carves into your soul, the more joy and significance you can contain—or that failure is an incubator keeping a premature success baby in a protective and controlled environment until it is ready to be birthed.

Many people become despondent about their lives and what things are occurring in them. They rarely give themselves a fair chance at accomplishing their goals because they will not acknowledge that their attempts to achieve them are frail. This is inevitably followed by a "woe is me" victim mentality, yet such a mentality is unfounded when they know their efforts are mediocre at best. They believe in their heart of hearts that they really cannot achieve what they are attempting. It's not that people with a "woe is me" mentality believe these things can't be done; they just don't believe that *they* can do the things they desire to do.

What happens when people's actions don't match with their expectations? The answer is nothing, really—except that their expectations are reduced to nothing but a wish! Nothing happens because their actions negate what they commit to verbally. Once people speak out from the depths of their true beliefs, not only from the superficial thoughts of their mind, their responses are called "reactions." These reactions are not simply a response to what they say; they are subsequent effects of their core belief in what they said. When what you think actually makes an eighteen-inch drop from your head to your heart is when you will began to see a real change in your life and actions.

Do you often find yourself verbally committing to the things you want to happen in your life and business, but you fail in your consistency to make them happen?

Here is what I want you to do. I want you to dive deeper. I want you to leave your ordinary and break through the serene surface of your safe place. Allow yourself to be alone with the true you. You may initially be amazed, but also confused. You will be able to see all the talents and gifts hiding inside of you, and they will bewilder you. Although this great, awesome potential resides in you, you can't fully comprehend why your life is presently where it is.

This is where I come in. My whole aim is to help you acknowledge the contradictory speech pattern woven throughout your life that makes it move in the direction it's moving. This will encourage you to move to the next phase of destroying those negative patterns and producing new patterns, which will lead you to a place of fulfillment and significance.

There are four dos on my list that you should follow to change your contradictory patterns:

1. **Success should be lived, not sought after.**
   I'm sure you've heard the expression, "Success is a journey, not a destination." It's true—however, what comes at the end of living successfully is having no regrets. You will be surprised what a plan will do for you, despite how brief the plan is. It doesn't matter if your plan is in brief sentences or written on a napkin from the coffee shop. Having any plan is better than having no plan at all. Don't seek success; follow a plan.

2. **Stop watching from the sidelines and get into the game.**
   If you allow fear to take root, you begin to doubt and sink into despair. By facing these fears head on, you open yourself to experiencing your real intrinsic potential, and you enable yourself to accomplish things that can only be accomplished while in the game.
3. **Take full responsibility of your life.**
   You must—not should—take ownership of every moment of your life . . . do not allow a second to slip by without placing in it the potential and creativeness to produce something for the next moment. Pack a punch so you are ready for every opposition that challenges you during the course of your day.
4. **Connect with a community of like-minded individuals.**
   You cannot grow spiritually unless you are willing to connect relationally. A tree cannot grow until a seed is planted in the dirt. A lightbulb can't shine until it is connected to a power source. To stand alone and live only for yourself is not only incomprehensible, but self-destructive as well.

I believe the foundation for wisdom is reading the Good Book, and there are two things it tells us to study—study to be quiet and study to know God's word. If we study to be quiet, we will know when not to speak. If we study to know God's word, we will know what to say when it is time to speak. This knowledge is imperative for transforming verbal commitments into planned action.

One of my personal client protégés, whom I have mentored for a number of years, was experiencing some problems that affected his personal vision for his life and business. Before a part of his world seemed to crash, Stanley (a fictitious name) was riding high on the success train. He was a young man who had experienced real success for the first time. He had dreams, and he was actually living them until his family life fell apart.

Stanley lost his home, his car, and, it appeared, his dignity. He kept me abreast of how things were going in his life, and I gave him small gold nuggets of advice for life and business to cash in for a return. One day, I subtly said to him, "Stanley, your actions aren't lining up with your expectations. What you *would* do is viewed as what you *should* do, but it has not reached the status of what you *must* do."

Seeing him a month later at a function, I noticed that something appeared to have clicked with him, because it was obvious that he was seeing his life and business differently. He later shared with me that he had decided to do one important thing—he made a firm decision.

Once he decided what he really wanted, there was nothing keeping him from getting it. He displayed a strong sense of resilience, and he refocused his mind and heart. His business was about to take off once again. And, while things were on an upswing, the new lady of his life walked out of his dreams and into his arms.

In a matter of a couple of years, he was able to buy a new home, buy new cars for he and his wife, and gain a new lease on life. Stanley's business went from handling a few hundred thousand to over $50 million.

Whenever you are going through something challenging in your life, never allow your current temporary circumstances to cause you to make permanent decisions about the rest of your life. I'm sure Stanley was embarrassed to some degree about what was happening, but he was not so embarrassed as to run away from those who cared about him and could really help him.

CHAPTER SIX

Back on Track

"We all want progress, but if you're on the wrong road, progress means doing an about-turn and walking back to the right road; in that case, the man who turns back soonest is the most progressive."
—C. S. Lewis

Getting life back on track is as simple as getting off of the train you're on and getting on the right one.

A FEW YEARS AGO, a young man from the United States decided to visit his sister who was living in France. He assumed that most of the French people he encountered would speak English. He soon discovered that many people spoke only their own language, and this included the ticket inspector on the train. The train inspector punched his ticket and then chatted cordially for a bit, making several expansive gestures. The young man simply nodded from time to time to show him that he was interested.

When the ticket inspector had gone, an American tourist also on the train leaned forward and asked if the young man spoke French.

"No," he admitted.

"Then that explains it," she said, "why you didn't bat an eyelid when the ticket inspector told you that you were on the wrong train."

Train tracks are designed to take a train to a particular destination. The train is intended to travel only on railroad tracks. The train cannot take short cuts, it cannot cut through fields, and it cannot change its course without the conductor. Even if the conductor changes the direction of the train by switching the tracks, the train maintains its position on the train tracks. Usually the result of a train that jumps the track is catastrophic.

Think of it this way: Who in their right mind buys a ticket to nowhere? If you would not buy a ticket to nowhere, why would you gamble with your life by getting on a train that is not even on a track? The tracks of success in any area of life are supposed to take the train's passengers to a place of success. If the train tries a route or speed that makes it skip the tracks, it has become derailed. Your journey becomes disrupted, upset, spoiled, or a major catastrophe.

Nine out of ten people who talk about how much their lives need fixing usually end up saying, "But I don't know where to begin." Oftentimes, however, it's not that they don't know where to begin; it's just that they are intimidated about starting in the place where they truly lost control. It takes a lot to give up control over something they created, even if it is a mess. These people will continue to lie to themselves until the evidence of the mess they've created is blatant. As long as the mess of accumulated things is disorderly stored in the closet, they will always feel as if it's not that bad.

⁓

Have you taken a good, honest, hard look at where your life is as opposed to where you want your life to be? Is your life on schedule according to your plans, or are your delays causing you to get further and further behind? Sometimes, you don't realize how far you have gotten away from the things you used to do and the person you used to be until you look back to see how far off track you are. Catching up may mean that you have to work harder, but the momentum and focus to make it happen, if you maintain them, will propel you ahead of schedule.

When your life begins to look a lot like a disorganized, cluttered closet, the first place to start getting back on track is with the thoughts in your head. To a great extent—more than you may want to realize or admit—your closet is demonstrative of your life. If your closet is messy, most likely your life is as well. If your closet is cluttered, your mind is most likely filled with things that you should let go. Yet you continue to hold on to them. Do not make the attempt to convince yourself that you don't have enough time or enough energy to correct your mess, but force yourself to make this small fundamental change, and it may reap large rewards in your life!

There is a story about a young man who had a promising career as a musician and photographer, but he had a partying lifestyle for years. He was an intravenous drug user and became severely addicted to methamphetamines. Eventually, his using was out of control and he was near death. He had been arrested and was on probation. If he got arrested again, he was going to be in prison for a very long time. The gig was up. He knew something had to happen or he was going to be that way forever. He realized he needed help.

He did not have the control over his problem that he assumed he had, so he entered a men's treatment program for help. He learned that he had probably been depressed most of his life. He also suffered from an anxiety disorder. He knew that anxiety and depression were issues that a lot of men in recovery have in common. Stimulants tend to be an antidote to anxiety, so before, when he would become depressed and anxious, he would gravitate toward stimulants as his drug of choice. In treatment, he identified and acknowledged his problem.

He no longer knew what he was going to do with his life when he entered this men's treatment program; he just knew he needed to follow the rules, and that meant getting on track. While at the men's treatment center, he started riding bicycles again. He noticed that there was a couple of old junk bikes that had been left at this men's facility, and the program manager was okay with some of the men working on the bikes in the garage. Many of the men in the treatment center had lost their licenses and couldn't drive, so having access to bikes provided them with some form of transportation with which to look for work. He started fixing more and more bikes and soon became known around the center as "the bicycle man." Today, he owns his own bike repair shop! His life was pretty complicated when he struggled with drug addiction, but he's back on track now. He's back to being the father that he always knew he could be. He is now able to sustain positive relationships, and he's able to own and operate a small business with a team of people. If he can do it, so can you!

The secret to getting back on track is finding the track to get on, and this starts with seeing and acknowledging your life's current derailments. When you can acknowledge derailments, you can demolish them. This first step to turning things around, although painful, is absolutely necessary.

For example, if your closet is in disarray, the first thing to do is remove all of your belongings and pile them on your bedroom floor. Once every last item has been removed from your closet (or storage unit or hallway closet or wherever it is that you store things), take a good look at the pile; how much of it is items you can no longer fit in or that you no longer use? Look at the clothing that you have been holding onto because you convinced yourself that it may come back in style. These clothes perfectly illustrate one of the lies you have told yourself in order to hold onto stuff you should let go.

Remember, *what you refuse to let go of becomes the junk in your life.* This method of examining your derailments and ridding yourself of junk applies not only to your material possessions, but to every aspect of your life. Bad habits that are at first too weak to notice become too strong to change—or at least seemingly so—but this change is necessary to get your life back on track.

For example, if one of your derailments is how you handle your finances, try this: collect all your bills, sit down at your kitchen table, and pile them up. Count them by comparing them to your income. You will be able to see, in the black and white reality of numbers, why you are experiencing financial troubles. Yet many are too afraid to confront the error of their ways, because if they truly discover the reason for their financial shortfall, they will not legitimately have any reason to complain. The last time I checked, complaining was not considered a strategy, but a travesty. Don't be afraid to look at the mess you've created. Own up to it because this will be the only way you can truly start to get your life back on track.

After you make your discovery of the junk—material or habitual—you have held onto, you may feel like screaming because of how ugly everything looks. Don't worry! It is often necessary to look back in order to move forward; it is not an indication that you have intentions on going back. To the contrary, taking an honest, retrospective look can help you recognize and avoid falling into the same snares that previously caught you unaware. It is important to know what to get right, so that you won't get it wrong again.

These instances in your life that are so often seen as markers to indicate the end of your life should be viewed rather as the end of an episode. Why pass judgment on the rest of your life based on one tragedy or one situation? Acknowledging the junk in your life can become an indicator of the end of a chapter, not the end of your life.

I look forward to seeing your life back on the right track, and I know you feel the same way.

CHAPTER SEVEN

BECOME AN ACTION FIGURE

"I don't know how tall I am or how much I weigh. Because I don't want anybody to know my identity. I'm like a superhero. Call me Basketball Man."
—LeBron James

Greatness is not what comes out of the womb of a woman; greatness is birthed out of the courageous heart that refuses to relent and does anything to stand and fight when faced with insurmountable challenges, even when initially afraid.

W<small>HEN I WAS ABOUT FOURTEEN YEARS OLD</small>, one incident changed my thoughts of who I was and what I could do. I was walking home from school one day, and I saw these three boys beating up this passive kid who wouldn't fight back. I don't know what came over me, but before I realized what I was doing, I spoke out and said, "Why don't you all leave this guy alone? Does it take all three of you to jump this kid?" It was almost like someone else was speaking out of my mouth, but it wasn't me. Unfortunately, it was, and I just invited myself into a fight.

The leader of the three had a reputation for being a troublemaker. He thought because he knew karate that he had the right to beat up on people who were afraid of him. Well, I became his next mixed martial arts challenge, which I did not officially sign up for. My mouth got me into another fine mess, but this time, I had to fight my way through it.

The guy said that he would fight me, and so I obliged him with the opportunity. As I was taking off my jacket to fight, the guy tried to hit me in my stomach. I moved just enough to avoid the blow, and I took my jacket off. I was angry that he would try to hit me while I was taking off my jacket, and without any forethought, I commenced beating this guy like he stole something from me. As we were fighting outside of a tavern, people came out to watch the fight. I was amazed that none of the adults watching the brawl tried to stop it. Nevertheless, I continued knocking him down and allowing him to get up, only so that I could knock him down again. The guy was bleeding profusely from the nose, and finally I asked him if he had had enough; the bully had no more fight left in him.

Personally, I felt that no lesson was taught and that fighting was overrated. However, I gained a sense of heroic accomplishment, because for the first time in my life, I helped to defend someone other than myself. After this incident, I still wasn't Superman or Hercules; I was just Mikel doing what I had never done before.

This one incident brought a major shift in my life, causing me to see myself and the people around me differently. I understood that I needed to control my environment, not people. I was ready for life. I was ready to accept responsibility for my actions and my future. This one incident was so profound in my life that it was the reason for a major transition in my self-confidence.

We have all experienced, in some form or another, abuse in our lives from friends, relatives, parents, and even ourselves, in the form of self-inflicted wounds, which has left an indelible mark on our psyche and, for some of us, our bodies. Despite every effort to erase these marks, they appear to be so deeply ingrained that they are impossible to remove. I believe that these scars are not meant to be removed, but to move us from the place where these scars were first engraved on our bodies and/or our minds. Yes, even Jesus, when He was resurrected, maintained the same wounds in His hands and feet as when He was nailed to the cross.

Have you ever had to be brave when you didn't want to be? So afraid, yet valiant? You realized, deep down to the core of your being, that you had to face your fears because you couldn't run from them anymore. It wasn't that you were tired of running from them; there was just no other place you could hide—not even within yourself. You just could not go on lying to yourself about your situation. You woke up and realized that all your friends were fully aware of your apprehension to confront your situation; they were just too nice to say anything to your face about it.

The fears I am talking about are not necessarily big monsters that stand ten feet tall with incredible strength. However, these fears are indeed giants of great size and power in your mind. These fears can be identified as excess weight, failure, loneliness, insecurity, low self-esteem, fear of starting a business, doing what you really want to do, etc. This list is practically endless, and only you know what fears actually exist inside of you. Ambrose Redmoon said, "Courage is not the absence of fear, but rather the judgment that something else is more important than fear."

If you are going to strip yourself of your Clark Kent suit of mediocrity, you cannot have a Plan B. Your Superman suit would be too large for such a frail body. Plan B should never be considered an option in case Plan A doesn't succeed. Plan B should only be considered as your next step, not your next plan, after Plan A has already been accomplished. Sequence is important for a systematized process for success, and Plan B is not a substitute.

Never be afraid to discover your strengths and use them to become your own version of an action figure. As Bo Bennett put it, "Every day, people settle for less than they deserve. They are only partially living, or at best living a partial life. Every human being has the potential for greatness." I understand how a person can feel everything but invincible when it comes to facing challenges. However, your strength is not hidden in your feelings, which are ever changing, but in your heart. Align your heart and mind, and your actions will mirror your thoughts.

The mild-mannered reporter, Clark Kent, was also Superman, and the millionaire playboy, Bruce Wayne, was actually Batman. What hero is lying around inside of you, waiting for the opportunity to come out and annihilate your fears? Go ahead, get up if you've been knocked down, and champion your own comeback. It's your life, and you have a right to not surrender to defeat if you don't want to. Remember, you can keep your name, but you can change your title . . . from victim to victor. Go ahead, make it happen! Life is waiting for an interview.

My experiences while growing up throughout the 1960s as a young boy were filled with dreams of being able to fly like Superman, swim like Aquaman, have a physique like Hercules, and have money like Bruce Wayne. I cannot recall one single friend while growing up who didn't imagine himself at one time or another as one of these action figures.

Those days were filled with innocent ambition and wonders that made life burst with fun. But all that began to change during my teen years. The challenges were real, the fights were unwarranted by bullies, my schoolwork became more like a contest to keep up, and insults were horrendous and at times mentally crippling. Instead of being Superman, I was Clark Kent, with little or no respect. I had the body of a stick instead of the physique of Hercules, and my family was considered poor by national statistics.

These negatives didn't keep me from dreaming. In fact, they made it all the more imaginably real as a possibility that my life would get better over time. These negative points in my past actually became indicators of turning points in life.

I believe that turning points are moments where transformation occurs for better or for worse, good or bad. We experience many of these turning points in our lives whenever we shift directions in order to make a decision or to avoid one. Perhaps it can be a decision about a relationship or what interests to pursue or the choice to stand up for something or someone. Maybe it is an educational or career choice, or the most beautiful person in school looks at you for the first time and you frost like a popsicle.

Some turning points are conscious; others less so. Some transitional moments may be imposed by family or other persuasive people in our lives. However, all transitional movements involve turning away from one lane and toward another. These twists and turns in life shape your identity and give you the experiences that come to define you along the way.

One young lady told me, "The turning point for me, in my life, was when I woke up and decided life was too short to live in a state of constant negativity. There were several steps I took, and it did not happen overnight. I had to constantly work at it, but NOW, I am completely positive, and with clearing out the bad, I discovered my true happiness that has been buried underneath all that negativity. I have a new great attitude and love to live each day to the fullest. I am more motivated and know that this is a much better place to be. I just wish I could help other people get to this place, but it is not for me to decide others' fates. Each person has to make the conscious effort to get here on their own. I am just here to tell them how wonderful it is on this side!"

Are there challenges that you have been afraid to confront because you feel that if you get into a fight with them you will lose? Are you still facing those extra thirty-plus pounds that seem undefeatable? What about your dream business or tackling your debts or even getting rid of those bad habits that continue to earn no dividends? Despite the difficulties that seem to plague you, you can overcome them.

Conviction, confidence, and courage—what I call the three Cs—are the major forces that will propel the very least of us forward. It does not matter what your background is, or what your past sins were, or who your parents are; there is a hero who resides in you.

THE THREE CS TO FACING CHALLENGES

Allow me to expound on these three Cs for the sake of supplying you with the tools and knowledge that are necessary so that you will be able to tackle all your issues with certainty. A conviction is a belief or opinion that is held firmly. Confidence is the self-assurance or belief in your ability to succeed. And courage is the ability and the audacity to face danger, difficulty, uncertainty, or pain without being overcome by fear or being deflected from a chosen course of action.

There is a story in the Bible that most of us are familiar with concerning David and Goliath. In the story, the Philistine army had gathered for war against the nation of Israel. The armies were at a standoff, with no one moving toward the opposing army. David, who was just a young teenager at the time, was sent by his father to the battle lines to check on his older brothers and bring back news to the family of their well-being.

David was a little bit different than the average person. He was accustomed to challenges because he had to protect his father's sheep by confronting and killing wild animals, such as a lion and a bear. He was the kind of person, even from a young age, who was willing to stand alone, if he had to, to stand on his conviction.

David had full intentions to do exactly what his father asked him to do. He showed up expecting to make sure his brothers were okay, get a few details about the progress of the battle, and return home with the news. However, the thing about people like David is that they are always open to whatever comes their way and don't automatically fall in line with the way everyone else thinks about or sees challenges.

The situation concerning the two opposing armies was apparently clear. The Philistines had Goliath, a self-confident giant warrior who had built quite a reputation in battle for killing thousands of men. He had always been the winner, and the Israelites were clearly intimidated and afraid of him. Israel obviously assumed that the Philistine army, along with Goliath, had the clear advantage—but not so according to David.

Each army was arranged on opposing sides of the valley. Whoever made the first move would be at a strong disadvantage, completely vulnerable to the opposing army. Each side was waiting for the other to attack. There Goliath stood, taunting the Israelites, trying to get them to make the first move.

When David came along, he brought with him a different viewpoint. He had never been involved in a battle such as this before, so he wasn't bound and mentally preprogrammed to think according to their unauthorized rules of battle.

David didn't know or care about Goliath's previous victories. David was a shepherd and had years of experience protecting his father's flocks from predators. To him, fighting Goliath was no different than battling a wild animal. David had God on his side as a shepherd, and he knew God was on his side that day as well. After David heard all of Goliath's insults against the army of Israel and their God, he said enough was enough and volunteered to fight Goliath.

The first thing King Saul offered after he allowed David to fight Goliath was to give David the weapons and armor that everyone else used. In other words, David was being hard-pressed to operate according to predetermined, yet unspoken rules of battle. They said, "This is the armor we always wear, and this is how you should battle Goliath."

Even as a young, inexperienced man of war, David was no idiot. He knew he wouldn't have a chance to defeat Goliath if he fought Goliath according to their rules of engagement. David understood that what was needed was something they had not seen in battle—a fresh perspective and an unconventional weapon.

David went against Goliath with the tools he knew best, instead of using King Saul's armor and sword, which were too heavy and unproven by him. The giant warrior laughed at David for coming to a fight with his childish appearance and toy-like weapon. However, David was not afraid, nor was he concerned with the giant's slanderous remark that his slingshot and rocks were inadequate. David did not take Goliath's threats as insults against himself, but against his God. So David ran toward Goliath with three things:

1. a positive mental attitude (Conviction),
2. a positive oral confession (Confidence), and
3. a rock in his slingshot (Courage).

David reached into his sack of five smooth rocks, pulled out his slingshot, loaded one of those rocks into his slingshot pouch, and hurled that rock toward Goliath's head. Suddenly Goliath's laughter was silent. Within just seconds, Goliath lay dead.

That wasn't enough for David. He picked up the sword of the fallen giant warrior, stood over him, and cut off Goliath's head. Then he lifted the head of the fallen giant so that the Philistines and the army of Israel could see and know that Goliath was dead. God must have looked down from heaven and said, "Now, this is a young man who knows how to get *a-head* in life!"

That's all it took. David knew who he was, what his strengths were, and how he could gain the advantage, and so must you. Just as David's did, your convictions will give way to confidence, your confidence will lend itself to courage, and your courage will create the audacity to act on your convictions.

Just as David did not drag Goliath's past victories into the equation when going into battle, so, too, you cannot pay attention to your opponent's history—for, in fact, what does their history have to do with your battle?

Just as David did not give way to the pressure of others' ideas of how to win, so, too, should you be willing to approach things differently. People who try to offer advice oftentimes are giving you information on how something has always been done. Why should you consider using their "armor" and "weapons of war" when they are too afraid to use them? My advice to you is to be like David—never take advice from a coward or someone who is afraid to fight.

David's final act of victory, cutting off Goliath's head, taught me a valuable lesson about combating my nemesis. Whether the enemy is excess weight, business apprehensions, social or close inner-circle relationship challenges—once the enemy is down and out, make sure it can never come to haunt you again by cutting off its head.

For David, the head of Goliath became his trophy. What trophies do you have from your victories? What trophies do you want to have?

As a final word of encouragement on the topic of action figures, I'd like to include the lyrics of a song sung by Mariah Carey that became extremely popular. In fact, the lyrics of this song really reach to the soul of a person who may be struggling and looking for a little extra push. I can personally identify with these words because of the doubts that I had in my abilities while growing up in Chicago. It's funny; I knew what I could do, but for some reason, I was too afraid to do it until I intentionally made up my mind that I was not going to remain the same person from that moment forward.

With this mindset, I was able to launch one of my restaurants and fight through all the obstacles that stood in my path to financial success. The principles I followed led me to the money to start my first restaurant, and that was just the beginning. May these words offer you the same type of inspiration.

"Hero" by Mariah Carey

There's a hero,
If you look inside your heart,
You don't have to be afraid of what you are,
There's an answer,
If you reach into your soul,
And the sorrow that you know will melt away.

[chorus]

And then a hero comes along,
With the strength to carry on,
And you cast your fears aside,
And you know you can survive,
So when you feel like hope is gone,
Look inside you and be strong,
And you'll finally see the truth
That a hero lies in you.

It's a long road,
When you face the world alone,
No one reaches out a hand for you to hold,
You can find love,
If you search within yourself,
And the emptiness you felt will disappear.

Turn on Your Life

[chorus]

Lord knows,
Dreams are hard to follow,
But don't let anyone tear them away,
Hold on,
There will be tomorrow,
In time you'll find the way.

That a hero lies in . . . you.

CHAPTER EIGHT
RETHINK POSSIBLE

"We all have possibilities we don't know about. We can do things we don't even dream we can do."
—Dale Carnegie

Some things will never be realized as long as you continue to say you cannot do them or you don't deserve them. But as soon as you say you can do something and that you deserve it, everything in you will look for a way to do it.

There once was a pastor who had a church member who would provide him with a rose boutonnière to pin on the lapel of his suit every Sunday. Because he always got a flower on Sunday morning, he really did not think much of it. It was a nice gesture that became routine. One Sunday, however, what he considered an ordinary day became very special.

As he was leaving the Sunday service, a young boy approached and said, "Sir, what are you going to do with your flower?" At first the pastor did not know what the boy was talking about, but then he understood.

"Do you mean this?" he asked as he pointed to the rose pinned to his coat.

"Yes, sir," the boy said. "I would like it if you are just going to throw it away. I'm going to give it to my granny. My mother and father got divorced last year. I was living with my mother, but I could not stay, so she sent me to live with my grandmother. She has been so good to me that I want to give that pretty flower to her for loving me."

The pastor could hardly speak. His eyes filled with tears, and he knew he had been touched in the depths of his soul by this young boy. He reached up and unpinned his flower. With the flower in his hand, he looked at the boy and said, "Son, that is the nicest thing I have ever heard, but you can't have this flower; because it's not enough."

The young boy looked surprised. But the pastor finished by saying, "If you'll look in front of the pulpit, you'll see a big bouquet of flowers. Different families buy them for the church each week. Please take those flowers to your granny because she deserves the very best."

The little boy grinned widely. "What a wonderful day! I asked for one flower but got a beautiful bouquet."

It may surprise you a bit, but life holds more for you than you can anticipate. Just because you may have experienced difficult times doesn't mean that you are destined to scrape the bottom of the barrel. And having made bad decisions or mistakes is not the finality of your life. Mistakes can be turned into little miracles if you learn to think differently.

This chapter is very dear to my heart, because I know what it's like to look at a seemingly impossible situation, to feel undeserving of something, and to have to fight every negative thought to believe that what I want is actually possible. It is possible to believe for more, even if you only asked for the little you think you can get.

What do you consider to be the biggest mistake you've ever made, and why do you think you made it? Would you like to learn how to avoid making blunders that would continue to mark your life?

I believe that in the next few moments, as you implement the principles from this chapter, you can overcome some of the hindrances that prevent you from succeeding. How many great inspirational ideas do you think you have had, but that you have never taken the liberty of putting to work? You would be surprised at the number of great ideas you have come up with that could have dramatically changed your life and income.

Ideas can easily slip away through passive focus. People can know what they want to do, but they may not realize what they have to do until their situations become critical. This is where most people are in life and business, and until they learn how to strike a balance between aptitude and attitude, they will continue to live their lives out of balance. Mistakes can easily hide out in the spheres of situations right before they hit critical status.

Do you feel like your life is slipping away? Are you receiving the return you expected on your most important asset—your time? Tuning in to specific principles can help you rethink the critical processes that create and nurture a culture of excellence and a culture defined by your personal, family, or organizational vision, mission, and values, rather than a culture that occurs by default.

Turn on Your Life

This is the age of knowing what you're made of, and it's time to rethink possible. If there is such a thing as "un-thinking" something, this is the time to do it. To un-think essentially means to unlearn. In fact, it is the process of ridding your mind of the knowledge or memory of something or to literally break the habit or end the practice of something. Un-think impossible and then rethink possible. Own up to your mistakes and do not ignore your mediocrity so that you can retool your life and business to conquer your opposition.

If time is in the constant mode of change, it is no small wonder that people, mentalities, businesses, technology, money, and how it's made are constantly evolving. Everything around you is changing—why aren't you? Some people retire mentally long before they retire physically. How can you expect to be great without doing anything great? Whether you are the head of a business, the head of your own company, or the head of your family, to drown in a pool of "I do not know what to do" is not an option.

People do not drown because they fall into water that is over their heads; people drown because they stay in water over their heads. The first thing people entering deep water need to know is not to panic; only then can they relax their minds and bodies and float.

In the same vein, to never have learned how to swim doesn't mean that you don't know how to swim. A person didn't know how to drown until he or she drowned. Therefore, you may not realize that you can upgrade your life, compete with your competition in business, or change your financial situation until you actually do it. To never have learned something is not an excuse to never do it. You can do what you have not learned. Learning to do something is simply realizing what you could have done all along. Learn to rethink possible!

My first experience rethinking possible was in 1981. I was in the army, stationed at Fort Ord, California. A friend asked if I was interested in going ice-skating with him. He asked me if I had ever ice-skated before, and I told him that I hadn't, but that I believed I could. My friend laughed.

"How do you know you can ice-skate if you have never done it?" he asked.

"Because I believe I can! Besides, I see myself skating on the ice," I replied. Again he laughed and went on to inform me of how long it took him to learn how to ice-skate and how difficult it was to first stand on those thin blades and move. I didn't care what he said—I knew what I could do, down to the core of my being. Don't ask me how I knew it; I just had an intuitive knowing.

When we arrived at the ice-skating rink, I put on the rented ice skates for the first time in my life. I didn't think that I had anything to prove, but my friend certainly did. In my mind, I had ice-skated time after time again. I saw myself going backward and turning, having fun on the ice. My friend put his skates on first and went onto the ice. With grace, he started skating. I could tell that he certainly knew what he was doing.

"Brown, hurry up!" he yelled at me. With great anticipation, I went onto the ice and actually glided and turned, without falling. I starting skating backward, and he looked at me with amazement.

"You lied to me. You said that you never ice-skated before," he said. I told him that I wouldn't lie about such a thing. Although I had never actually ice-skated before, my belief that I could was stronger than my lack of experience.

Whoever said that you cannot do something that you've never done was lying. People do things they've never done all the time. It is a matter of believing that if you do not have the experience, you can figure it out in a relatively short amount of time. I figured that riding a bicycle could be no different from riding a motorcycle. One has a motor to move the cycle, and the other needs your legs and feet. In either case, it is about balance, not the bike.

When Henry Ford decided to produce his famous V-8 motor, he chose to build an engine with the entire eight cylinders cast in one block and instructed his engineers to produce a design for the engine. The design was placed on paper, but the engineers agreed, to a man, that it was simply impossible to cast an eight-cylinder engine-block in one piece. Ford replied, "Produce it anyway."

People with ordinary thinking and beliefs will only attempt to achieve things that involve little or no risk and that involve as little resistance as possible because the fear of failure controls their lives. However, the person who thinks the impossible is possible is simply an ordinary person with extraordinary belief that all things are possible for those who believe.

I made up in my heart and mind to rethink possible. You should, too.

CHAPTER NINE

BELIEVE IN YOURSELF

"Believe in yourself! Have faith in your abilities!
Without a humble but reasonable confidence in your
own powers you cannot be successful or happy."
—NORMAN VINCENT PEALE

*People often see extraordinary qualities in others,
but are oftentimes blind to their own intrinsic qualities.*

THERE IS A STORY OF A MAN who went in search for truth. The first man he came across was an old religious man sitting under an old tree, just outside his own village. He said to the man sitting under the tree, "I am searching for the True Master. Can you tell me his characteristics?"

"His description is very simple," the old man said. "You'll find him sitting under an old tree, sitting with his legs crossed, his hand under his chin . . . that is enough to know he is the True Master."

The seeker started searching. Thirty years passed while he wandered the whole earth. He visited many places but never met anyone whom he considered to be the True Master. He met many masters and learned something from each of them, but none were the True Master. Early in his search, he came across a little boy who he told about his quest for the True Master. The little boy became intrigued with his story and wanted to know more, but the man had to leave to continue in his search.

At long last, the man returned to his own village, completely exhausted. As he returned he was surprised—he could not believe—that the tree under which the old man once sat was still there. Reminiscing on all the time he had spent searching for the True Master, he sat under the same tree where the old man once sat.

The man felt a sense of disappointment; he had never found the True Master. But while he was sitting under the tree with his legs crossed and his hand under his chin, a man walked up to him and bowed on the ground, repeatedly calling him, "True Master, True Master."

The man sitting under the tree said, "Why are you calling me True Master?"

The man bowing before the old man said, "Thirty years ago, when I was just a boy, a man told me how he would know if he found the True Master. He would be sitting under an old tree with his legs crossed and his hand under his chin, and so here you are!"

The man sitting under the tree suddenly had a revelation. The religious old man, who had told him how he would find the True Master, simply saw in him what he could not believe and see in himself.

HEART-LEVEL BELIEFS

When you feel as if you have nothing to offer or you are unworthy of things, it is an indication that you may be struggling with a self-image defect. Therefore, it is difficult to see and believe in your internal qualities because your view of yourself is always in review instead of preview. However, you are worthy and you are capable. Instead of using valuable time thinking the worst about yourself, use that energy to think the best about yourself. If you're having trouble seeing all of the remarkable things about you, one good way to change your personal view and start building your confidence is to not compare yourself with others.

Are you blind to your intrinsic qualities and strengths? If you have low self-esteem, harness the power of your own thoughts and beliefs to change how you feel about yourself. A low self-esteem can negatively affect virtually every facet of your life. You can take steps to boost your self-esteem, even if you've been harboring a poor opinion of yourself since childhood. Start with these three Bs, which are steps to a healthier self-esteem:

1. Believe in yourself. Recognize your strengths, even if you have to write all of them down. You have to be your own best friend, and then you can be a good friend to others.
2. Become conscious of your thoughts. Once you've identified troubling conditions or situations, pay attention to your thoughts about them. This also includes what you tell yourself—and your interpretation of what and why you feel a particular way.
3. Before you do anything else, repeat steps 1 and 2. Consistency is the strength of discipline. Developing consistency is not doing ten different things, but doing one thing well enough so that it can spill over into other parts of your life.

You do not have to make fifty things a priority; I am emphasizing that you really only have to do one thing—believe. When people believe the truth, at a heart level, a transformation happens in their lives apart from them working hard to make something happen.

A study was done in the late '70s that said that the most negative and destructive thing you can do to your self-worth is to try to "become." What I mean by this is that when you try to become something, you are making a silent statement to your heart that you are not whatever you are trying to become.

For example, if you say that I am going to try to become wealthy, you are saying to your heart that you are not wealthy. What you are doing is starting from a negative. In essence, those who made millions are no different from those who made only thousands. Both pulled out of their own talent and gifting based on what they believed to be true. Money doesn't come from without; it first comes from a heart of belief.

The truth of the matter is when you are deluded and full of doubt, even a thousand books or Bible scriptures are not enough. What you exhibit in your life is the way you really believe. And what you believe is simply what you are. The core of your belief is not exemplified in what you say, but rather in what is displayed by your actions. You are not defined by what you say; you are defined by what you do. Talking faith is not a true measure that you walk by faith.

Faith is to believe what we do not see, and the reward of this faith is to see what we believe. Out of the heart flow all the boundaries of your life. People are trying to get God to remove the boundaries, but God doesn't control the boundaries—you do. Your boundaries cannot be solved out there somewhere in space. The boundaries are in your heart! The boundary is that you have an inward, deep-seated belief about yourself and what you think you deserve.

Here is some good news . . . God is not mad at you! God loves you and He wants nothing more than to help you. God knows what He placed in you, but He is also aware of what limitations you place on yourself. And, for this reason, I would like to give you a message of hope and to offer you freedom from your mental bondage. The only way this can happen is by you allowing a revamp of your whole internal system.

As Ralph Waldo Emerson explained, "We are born believing. A man bears beliefs as a tree bears apples." The heart is the abode of deep beliefs. The beliefs of the heart are directly linked to our sense of self. It is the beliefs of the heart that determine our views of ourselves, God, and the world in which we live. If we renew our mind (pattern of thought) to see ourselves as creative beings, we can experience incredible realities. When we continue to see ourselves as we used to be, we replant those old seeds of limitations and fear that ruled our life.

So, what is that incredibly small change that can happen at the very core of a person's existence that will bring a dramatic and effortless transformation at every level? Simple! A change in the beliefs of the heart concerning how wonderfully you are made.

How much money do you have on you now? Go ahead and look in your pockets. Please don't include your credit cards, because they are simply borrowed money—unless, of course, your cards are secured by your own money. Well, did you count how much money is in your pockets? What about cash in your bank accounts and investments?

You can go through every source where you have money stored, invested, hidden, or even buried in your backyard, and still, that is not how much money you have. The amount of untold billions you possess is not in your hands. Think about it!

People have dared to count the apples on a tree, but who has the audacity to count the apples in the seed? *There is more money in your ability and talent than there is in your bank account.*

CHAPTER TEN

Choose All over Nothing at All

KEEP TRYING UNTIL YOU ACHIEVE IT

"Most of the important things in the world have been accomplished by people who have kept on trying when there seemed to be no hope at all."
—Dale Carnegie

Keep reaching until it's in your grasp; keep believing until you attain it; keep fighting until you conquer it; keep running until you reach the finish line; keep working until it's done; keep studying until you understand it; keep dreaming until you are living it; keep pursuing until you catch it; and keep practicing until you are almost perfect.

I know of two young men who started a restaurant on the north side of Chicago. They didn't have the necessary funds to start, but they had all the desire and fire. Their parents were telling them that it was a mistake. Their friends thought that it was a good idea, but for someone else with more experience. To add insult to injury, the area where they started was not the best economical place to start. The entire city of Chicago was experiencing an economic degeneration, and many families in that community were laid off their jobs. However, the brothers thought that it couldn't get any worse, so they pursued their dream.

They quickly discovered that dreaming the dream was easier than starting the business. Short on money, they decided to sell their cars and anything else they could to raise the necessary capital. They made up in their minds that it was all or nothing. They took the gamble and put everything into their business. The building they rented for the restaurant had an upstairs apartment that came with it, and they lived there because they could not afford to live anywhere else. The restaurant was launched, and like most restaurants, the first month was great. The second month was not bad, but by the third month business seem to slow down.

They almost gave up until they remembered what they had professed: "It's all or nothing." They then completed the phrase with, "It's all!" They took stock of everything they were not doing and everything that was right about what they were doing. The rest is history. They have since been featured on one of the shows on the Food Network because their restaurant has become one of Chicago's favorite places to eat.

I have spent the better part of my life working to better the lives of other people, reaching the up-and-out to the down-and-out, helping rocky marriages, and helping to launch rocketing careers. I have seen my share of challenges and treaties, defeats and triumphs.

Throughout them all, nothing can replace the accelerating feeling of being a part of helping someone finally reach the apex of his or her abilities.

On the other hand, I have experienced some huge letdowns, seeing such talented and gifted people strive to reach that all-too-elusive dream, but who then give up without realizing they were right at the threshold of success. These people didn't stop because they didn't have any more strength to continue; they gave up because they decided to quit. They walked away—stopped fighting in the middle of the round.

In retrospect, when I interviewed these people, I heard them give some of the oddest excuses for why they quit. One promising football player said he was tired of the coaches yelling at him. He felt humiliated and belittled, yet as Eleanor Roosevelt said, "No one can make you feel inferior without your consent."

"Do you know everything about the game and what you are supposed to do?" I asked this promising football player.

"No," he said.

"So," I replied, "what is in you that you cannot understand coaches are there to help you enhance your ability, to sharpen your skills, and to equip you with everything possible for you to be your best? If yelling is how they do it, remember they can easily replace you with someone willing to listen."

Another person admitted it was sheer fear of actually being successful and the cost to maintain it that caused him to quit. Mediocrity can be more attractive than success for some people, and a quitter doesn't have to search hard for excuses; they are everywhere. The dog ate my homework, I don't like dealing with the IRS, what if, it can't be done, too many people are in the line, I tried it, it doesn't work—and the list of excuses goes on and on like the Energizer Bunny.

If you really want to do something in your life, no excuse can be found; but when you really do not want to do something, any excuse will do. As George Washington Carver said, "Ninety-nine percent of the failures come from people who have the habit of making excuses." If you decide you want to start a business but you don't have all the money to start, start something with the money you have. Find a hundred dollars a month or five hundred every month, and save it for a year. Don't look at putting everything in place before you start; start with what you can muster up . . . no excuses. Follow the suggestion of Nike, and just do it! Yes, I'm yelling at you. Just do it!

Why are you deceiving yourself into inactivity by claiming that you only want to start at the top? No one starts a business at the top. This excuse is just a way to convince yourself that starting at the bottom is unacceptable, which has given you a reason not to do it. My friend, it is the "not starting" that is unacceptable. The only people who will begin at the top of their career field are grave diggers . . . and they will eventually find themselves in a hole.

Stop looking for reasons to quit. There are no returns if you invest in quitting. Find your dream and go after it like a cheetah running down its prey. And, while you are in hot pursuit of your dream, continue scanning your brain for reasons to keep moving on. If you start your business the right way and with the right attitude, you won't have to start it again.

THINK OF WHAT'S RIGHT WITH YOU
Have you ever been disturbed with your actions and said, "What's wrong with me!?" Well, this is a usual response to disappointment in personal performance. When you know you could have done better, don't downgrade yourself; instead, examine the degree of your effort. This is not a bad place to be, but rather a great disposition to

exhibit. It is not how things turned out that caused your distress; it's what you "said" to yourself after you saw your results. Instead of asking yourself what's wrong with you, ask yourself what's right with you. Don't be so quick to downgrade yourself when you can easily determine your strengths and reconsider other ways to accomplish your goals.

You can be at a great station in life and never recognize the benefits or the advantages of being there. When you fail to detect your current position, you will deplete the power of your leverage. If you only focus on the end result, you will become extremely disappointed with the results you produce because they won't quite measure up to your false expectations.

The rewards rarely ever match the gratifying feelings of knowing you did everything you could to accomplish your goal. Please don't misunderstand me as to think that the results are unimportant. That is not what I am insinuating. To hold the trophy at the end is an award, but overcoming the challenges along the way is a reward. How much you are giving in the effort depends on the passion you have for what you're doing.

Ladies, consider your appearance after once weighing 181 pounds and losing 45 pounds. And gentlemen, reflect on how your clothes fit you now, weighing 172 pounds, when you once weighed 235 pounds. The look is great, but the feeling is even greater. You feel healthier, you're off of your blood pressure meds, you can shop in department stores without the frustration of not finding clothes you like to wear, and you feel more confident about yourself as a result of what you do on a consistent basis to not only lose the weight but to maintain your weight loss. Even though the goal may have been met with your weight loss, your body has to be maintained.

It is all about the climb—the journey, the fight, and the exertion. The award is simply a trophy that you can place on your mantle;

however, discovering and developing your mental strength—or physique or creativity or whatever—is the reward that benefits you the most. The award is far less valuable than the personal reward. The award is the result of the accolades of people, but the reward is the enjoyment of the exertion of overcoming the personal struggle to finish.

Think of all the things that are right with you, and don't place a major focus on your negatives. The negatives can change into the positives as you change your perspective of them so that you will exert yourself with all fervor. You have all the right things stuffed down inside of you; it's just that sometimes your expectations don't quite match up to your true ability. Oftentimes, this happens when we have a propensity to measure ourselves by someone else. You are designed as a beautiful specimen, a masterpiece. Why would you fractionally use your creative ability based on someone else's ability? Get out of the comparing mode and stop competing with others. Why be concerned with how others may feel if you don't quite hit the home run in life? What others may want from you is usually what they don't expect out of themselves.

Be your own gauge! Don't prepare yourself based on what others may have achieved. Don't even consider giving your best effort, which is usually predicated on just above minimum requirement. Effectively becoming unattached from the results requires emptying yourself during your efforts. When you know you have nothing left in you after you have exerted yourself because of your passion for whatever it is you do, your climb will be worth more than accolades from others.

It always amazes me how most people are so preoccupied with potential results when they have not thus far even begun the effort. Before you begin anything, you should ask yourself, "Am I ready to be totally engaged in my effort to develop myself, my business, or am I just interested in taking the shortcuts so that I can get a satisfactory result for little personal investment?" Your priority should not be the results; your priority should be the passion required to exert yourself to the max.

You cannot work it out until you outwork yourself.

CHAPTER ELEVEN

Contract and Build the Life and Business of Your Dreams

"You are never too old to set another
goal or to dream a new dream."
—C. S. Lewis

*Low standards will always equate to poor
quality when it deals with construction.*

LIFE IS ABOUT BUILDING and finding the necessary tools to build the kind of life you really want for you and your family. However, there is one major disadvantage to doing it yourself (DIY). You may not know how to do everything to ensure life's construction goes smoothly and on schedule. When it comes to establishing and building a business, it is going to take as much grit as it does knowledge. Consider these brief abridgments of

Angie Hicks Bowman's and J. K. Rowling's stories of how they got started in their preferred fields.

Angie Hicks Bowman, founder of Angie's List—an online and phone service that helps consumers find ratings on local services—discovered success by building her business over time with quality data and ideas that have increased her subscribers into the millions. Not surprisingly, by connecting with millions of subscribers and running effective national TV commercials and radio ads, Angie's List is thriving—and so is Angie. Not only is she the founder of her company, but she is also the chief marketing officer, with an estimated net worth of $50 million.

Angie is an example of an individual who knows what she wants and who exercised her resilience to make her dreams come true.

J. K. Rowling is another person who sought after her dreams and achieved success. Rowling may be rolling in *beaucoup* dollars from her Harry Potter books and movies today, but before she published the series of novels she was nearly penniless, severely depressed, divorced, and trying to raise a child on her own while attending school and writing a novel. If that's not a lot on one's plate, I don't know what is. Although I do not advise people to do what Rowling did—using the company's computer while on the clock to write her novel—I respect her drive to follow through with the process. This successful author went from depending on welfare to being one of the richest women in the world in only a few years. J. K. Rowling admits that through her hard work and determination, Harry Potter was able to jump out of the books and onto the silver screen.

Usually, before I lay my head on the pillow, I ask God to help me dream my dreams. Two things I expect to happen when I fall asleep. One, I anticipate having a wonderful dream of my future; or two, I anticipate having a good night's rest. Both of these are extremely gratifying. In either case, I wake up refreshed and ready to put my plan into action.

In order to build the life of your dreams, you have to be able to dream of the life you would like to build. As Jim Rohn puts it, "If you go to work on your goals, your goals will go to work on you. If you go to work on your plan, your plan will go to work on you. Whatever good things we build end up building us."

Imagine that your life is like a building under construction, and you are the general contractor. You are the only one who is responsible for the end product. The general contractor ensures that all subcontractors (special tradespersons) understand all levels of their portions of the blueprints and the kinds of material that should go into the building, which makes you, the general contractor of your life, ultimately responsible for the outcome of the construction work. You have to hire subcontractors who are licensed, bonded, and well equipped to perform their part of the job. Just as general contractors would not allow inexperienced subcontractors to use substandard materials in their buildings, you cannot allow people to invest substandard things into your life.

Understand this: the kind of advice you listen to is as equally important as is whom you receive the counsel from. The people you respect and listen to have obviously been given the privilege to speak into your life as subcontractors, and you consciously or subconsciously authorize them to bring with them whatever quality or inferior thought materials they possess. Don't trust that people will not use the same worthless items they built their own lives with to help build yours.

You see, it works like this. People project and send subliminal messages that your subconscious mind picks up without you realizing what is transpiring. You may not want to see the faults in another person's life because your frontal brain is focusing on the respect you have for that person. However, your subconscious is taking in all the unscrupulous and defeating tendencies this person has.

Your subcontractors, just as at an actual construction site, have access to your construction site (life) because they are your mentors, teachers, ministers, friends, or associates. The same applies to whatever you choose to read; words are the building blocks of thoughts, and these notions are the wheels to your motions, and your motions are the good, bad, or indifferent actions of your life.

You can be subliminally misled into making decisions that are solely based on another person's thoughts and actions. People have missed out on millions of dollars and have literally walked away from what they were designed to do because they listened to someone who decided that what they should do was not worth the time and effort. Just because other people do not want to attend a wealth-building seminar or listen to the quality material you choose to listen to or attend a marriage seminar in order to better their marriages, don't let their unintentional messages slip into your subconscious and cause you to make choices that are in the long run damaging and restrictive.

People often get stuck in life with wasted materials they have collected along life's journey that others have used for their lives. Therefore, the life they were trying to build is actually the life of someone else. Whether it's your dream business, dream house, or dream spouse, your dreams must be what you want, not what someone else wants for you. You have no one else to blame for the house (life) you are now experiencing. You built it. If you don't like what your life resembles, renovate it with the kind of quality materials (thoughts) that will improve your life, finances, business, and marriage. You will be glad you did.

Build Your Dream

Do something extraordinary and watch your life change. Start with where you are to build the life of your dreams. What you have is not all you can have. What you do now is not all you are able to do. And what you know is not all you will ever learn.

What is the best investment you believe you can make that will immediately reap gigantic benefits both personally and monetarily? If your response is "in yourself," then you are absolutely correct. It's no secret that YOU are your greatest asset. Let's face it; you really are all that and a bag of chips.

Take a deep breath and plunge into the BEST YOU ever. It's time to get your game face on and bring your "A" game into the arena of life. It is time for you to stop *thinking* that you're good enough and start *believing* that you are good enough. Let your imagination soar and cross the threshold of mediocrity into the limitless sky. Now, for the first time, you can and will begin to experience life from a whole different perspective. You can live life on purpose, and not on accident. A proper introspection is far greater than a false perception.

In order to learn, you must first be taught. In order to experience what you have been taught, you must apply what you have been taught. In order to never return to the state of ignorance, you must constantly practice what you have been taught. Success is the antidote to failure, but success doesn't come without the right information. When your source of information becomes plugged up, abnormality sets in and your growth becomes stunted.

Allow me to share a story that will help explain what I meant by the statement above. One day I went bowling with a young protégé of mine in business. The young man was a novice when it comes to bowling, so he asked if I could teach him how to be a better bowler. I consider myself a decent bowler because I learned how to bowl from a person whose bowling average was about 220. The lessons I learned from my bowling mentor are what I try to teach whenever I have the opportunity to bowl with friends.

As we started bowling, I noticed several things he was doing wrong. I mentioned to him that when your methods are wrong, so it will be with your results. He was becoming more frustrated with his failure to get strikes, so I offered to give him some pointers. I sensed his willingness to listen and apply my instructions, and so I continued to enlighten him on how to better bowl. As he bowled each frame under my tutelage, he saw an immediate improvement in his game.

At this time, he was getting more strikes and spares, so I decided to stop giving him information because his score was getting too close for comfort. However, he noticed when I stopped instructing him, he quickly returned to his same old habits. At this time, it was no longer just a game, but a life lesson to teach. I said, "Remember what I said, don't watch the pins but rather the marking on the floor, and keep your shoulder from turning." I never had to say another word, because from that point on, he realized that the strikes and spares he was previously experiencing under my instructions, were a matter of rehearsing my words in his mind. My words became a part of his psyche, and he continued applying them to bowl a good score. Bowling for him was no longer a psychological game, but rather a psychological transformation.

Are you overscheduled and underrested? You can improve the quality of your life with the right strategies to free up time for what you really want to do. There are different ways to overcome goal-challenging weariness and to accomplish your objectives, which may seem like shortcuts to reach your goals. However, they really aren't shortcuts at all. These so-called shortcuts are simply better avenues and methods of doing something when you were originally using the long version or the wrong technique.

It all comes down to the kind of material and processes used to gain and have a happier and more fulfilled life. If you don't like what your thoughts are manufacturing in your life, inspect the kind of thoughts you are allowing to come into your psyche on a daily basis. Don't talk yourself into cutting quality while expecting better results. It's ludicrous to think that you can fill your mind with substandard thoughts and still produce quality actions. Your actions are the products of your thoughts.

Don't be afraid of your dream; and do not be ashamed of your present life. Your life, like most all things in this world, is subject to change. Where your life is now is not where it is going to end up. Start planning and start building, now!

CHAPTER TWELVE

DEVISE YOUR OWN AMAZING COMEBACK

"Success is going from failure to failure
with no loss of enthusiasm."
—WINSTON CHURCHILL

It takes a lot to come back after you have been knocked down numerous times by life—but then, you knew what the cost would be. That is the only reason you continue to get up and continue to fight, because you are willing to pay the price for your comeback.

STEPHENIE MEYER, the author of the *Twilight* series, said the inspiration for her book came to her from a dream. Once she received her inspiration, she applied her perspiration and finished writing her book in three months. She never intended to publish it until a friend suggested she should. She wrote about fifteen letters to literary agencies. Five of them didn't reply. Nine literary agencies just flat-out dismissed her book as an ordinary vampire novel. Only one company gave her a chance. Then eight publishers auctioned for the rights to publish *Twilight*. She got a three-book deal worth $750,000. In 2010, Forbes reported she earned $40 million. She was under forty years old at the time she wrote the first book.

⁂

Winston Churchill's quote at the beginning of this chapter may seem difficult and challenging, but the reality of life is that you are going to experience failure and disappointment, and how you handle it will be the difference between success and permanent failure. The person who doesn't make mistakes is unlikely to make anything.

Every failure is not a mistake and every mistake is not failure. Some mistakes serve to help narrow your options for what will work, which is good. However, with constant diligence, you will discover a way; and you will achieve success. One of my favorite successful characters to talk about is Thomas Edison. He said, "I have not failed. I've just found ten thousand ways that won't work." He was unrelenting in whatever he went after to achieve: "Of the two hundred lightbulbs that didn't work, every failure told me something that I was able to incorporate into the next attempt."

There are no shortcuts to any place worth going. There is no elevator to success; you are going to have to take the stairs. Each step gets you higher and closer to your goal. When someone says something can't be done, do it anyway. If you can't do it, then it doesn't exist. People do not become what they want to be without first wanting to become what they want to be. In other words, you cannot hit your target if you don't know what you are aiming for. You will always fail in your attempt to be someone you are not, but you will always succeed at being yourself.

There are many parasitical obstacles and challenges looking to eat away at your confidence and self-esteem. In order to shield yourself against these psychological arrows of attack, you must have a defense that is both resistant to these alluring deceptions and is prepared to defend you against these mental assaults. These seemingly insignificant thoughts are sometimes dismissed as harmless. To the contrary; these thoughts come with names such as fear, discouragement, frustration, anxiety, and doubt. All of these have the ability to cause the best of us to throw in the towel and declare defeat.

Momentary setbacks create opportunities for fresh commitment and renewal. They are transitory incidents that carry only the weight you give them. You will always have seasons of struggles and testing. There are times when everything you attempt to do will seem to go all wrong. Regardless of your prayers and dedication, adversity will come. The Apostle Paul of the Bible prayed three times to God about his thorn in the flesh, and God's answer was "My grace is sufficient." Some things are not meant for you to change, but to survive—you must outlast the struggle and live to tell the tale. If you can't alter it, then outlive it! You can't help at times being delayed, but faith will never be denied.

One of the greatest struggles you will encounter is the temptation to make permanent decisions based on temporary circumstances. Patience results from trust. So, allow me to give you some insights to help you survive the peaks and valleys of life. Dreamers are always surrounded by assassins trying to divert them from their course, to keep them broke, to keep them sick, to keep their marriage in constant disrepair, and to keep them in doubt. It is necessary, then, that you gather together all your mental faculties to prepare yourself to stand up and defeat every challenge that opposes you.

Steven Spielberg applied to the prestigious University of Southern California film school and was denied twice. Instead he went to Cal State University in Long Beach. He later went on to direct some of the largest grossing and biggest movie blockbusters in the history of cinema. Today, his net worth is over $3 billion, and in 1994 he received an honorary degree from the film school that rejected him twice.

There are three major points that will always propel you into prominence after you have been denied an opportunity to realize your dream.

1. A Denied Opportunity Is Not the Only Opportunity

You will always miss 100 percent of the shots you don't take, you will miss 100 percent of the questions on a test you don't answer, and you will never achieve 100 percent of the things you never do. Success favors the bold and the courageous. If you have never faced fear, embarrassments, disappointments, or hurt, it means you have never taken any chances. A chance is nothing but an opportunity, spelled differently. Opportunities are not always offered, but rather created and taken.

What do you do when you have been denied an opportunity? When you have been denied the chance to prove that you can do the job—or when, after a screen audition, a director instructs you to try your luck in a different occupation—or when you have been turned down by a banker who didn't take your business plan seriously—or when you have a career-ending knee surgery? You get up. It's that simple . . . but it's not that easy.

Remember, this is all about YOU right now! What is it that your heart truly desires right now? Achieving your dream job? Starting your bakery business? Learning something new to inspire you? Whatever it is, what are you waiting for?

Whoever turned your ideas down or told you to go back to the drawing board does not own opportunities—you do! Are you a teen or do you have a teen who dreams of a dance career, but you don't know how or where to begin? Are you a grandparent who really wants to take advantage of an opportunity to go back to school to get your college degree? Go for it! You own this moment; no one else does. You can choose to create an opportunity or take advantage of the one presented to you. The power is in your hands.

2. Find the Knowledge and Tools You Need

Assemble the knowledge you need to succeed. Look at your goals and identify the skills you'll need to achieve them. Then look at how you can acquire these skills by reading books, attending seminars covering your desired subject, and assertively moving forward with your newly discovered information. Working on you before working on others is not called selfishness; it's called self-development.

Don't accept a sketchy, just-good-enough solution—look for a solution, a program, or a course that fully equips you to achieve what you want to achieve and, ideally, gives you a certificate or qualification you can be proud of achieving. To start, visit my website, www.mikelbrown.com, which provides a list of books that are helpful to establish a footing in your endeavors and stories to read that will inspire you.

Start by doing the right things. By starting with small, easy wins, you will put yourself on the path to success and will start building the self-confidence that comes with knowledge.

3. Maintain Your Focus

It is important that you understand the process and that you don't reach for perfection. This will be the quickest way to frustration. Just enjoy doing simple things successfully and well. Maintain your focus by setting small goals and achieving them. However, do not become married to these small, comfortable goals that don't produce enough spark to be sustaining. Remember, you are making a comeback after experiencing a setback. Therefore, change the level of difficulty by challenging yourself with new goals.

I can recall an incident that occurred in 1982 when I was selling insurance for this particular agency. I was well trained by my general agents who, before I came on the scene, had made a lot of money. I remember their lavish homes and luxury vehicles that I assumed came as a result of their success in the insurance industry. They would often tell me that all they achieved, I could, too. I believed them and I worked hard. I would sell at times as much as five to ten life policies a day or twenty-five to thirty in a week. I was making money; at least I thought I was.

Later a problem arose that caused one of the agents to ask about a check he was supposed to receive but never got. I became a bit inquisitive, but I didn't pay too much attention because I was too busy selling. You see, for years the insurance company was paying everyone a salary and a commission, but nobody was getting their salary—because these sketchy people were taking the salary part for themselves. In the meantime, an investigation was going on. Of course, it was hush, hush.

I had made a name for myself because of how I sold tons of insurance policies, both life and health. Other agencies even asked me to come in to train their agents to sell more efficiently. I made a lot of money for both the agency and the insurance company, and when you make as much money as I made for them, you get noticed. During my developing time with the company, they decided to heavily invest in my education, for the purpose of promoting me to general agent over the agency to replace these two unscrupulous general agents, who they knew were under investigation for allegedly purchasing and distributing illegal substances.

As law enforcement was getting closer in their investigation, these two men left the country, thus leaving behind two vacant positions. When they abandoned their posts, the vice president of the insurance company called me in for a meeting. I assumed the company wanted to know if I was involved in their scandal. Instead, the VP told me that they had been watching my sales and asked if I would like to take over the agency. They were willing to give me half of the fourth floor of the bank building to reformat the agency. They informed me that I would be responsible for hiring and training the agents, and the agency would be named after me.

The remaining part of their offer wasn't too bad, either. They would give me all the monies due to me since my coming to the agency and give me a salary of XYZ thousands, the insurance company would pay all the agency expenses including salary plus commission for the agents, and I would receive a minimum of 50 percent commission on every policy sold by the agents.

When I first heard of what these two general agents had done to me and the other agents, I was angry. I could have become bitter against these guys I thought were my friends, but I refused. Just to think, they actually stole my paychecks and forged my name on checks that belonged to me. I made a conscious decision to move on. I believe that a person is better as they manage their mind by staying on top of their positive thinking patterns. Continue to celebrate and enjoy your victories, and strengthen those mental images that will ensure a united front against discouragement when things do not happen the way you expect or as fast as you would like.

Do not be afraid of failure. Learn how to handle it and use it to thrust you onto an altogether different level. Accept the reality that there will be times when what is attempted doesn't seem to work and that mistakes happen when you're undertaking something new. In fact, if you get into the habit of considering mistakes as learning experiences, you will start to see them in a positive light. After all, "If it doesn't kill you, it makes you stronger!"

CHAPTER THIRTEEN
DISARMING PRESSURE AND STRESS

"In times of great stress or adversity, it's always best to keep busy, to plow your anger and your energy into something positive."
—LEE IACOCCA

Stress and pressure can be fairly good motivators if they are handled correctly, but they don't have to control your emotions or behavior.

ONCE UPON A TIME there were two holy men strolling down a wooded path in a forest outside Naples, Italy. Their heads were tonsured and bowed, and the hoods of their robes cut much of the world off from view as they strolled along, softly mumbling their orisons.

Coming to a narrow stream, they stopped. A young lady stood beside the stream. She had on a new pair of shoes and a long peasant dress and seemed reluctant to cross the stream lest she muddy her garment. Without a moment's hesitation, one of the monks picked up the young woman and carried her across. He put her gently back down on the path. She smiled her thanks, and he nodded in response.

The two monks continued their walk, in silence now. After some time had passed, the other monk, who was obviously highly agitated, broke the quiet.

"How could you do that?" he asked, his face in a grimace of disapproval. The first monk, who had been deep in thought, looked at his companion in astonishment.

"Do what?" he asked.

"How could you touch that woman? You picked her up and handled her and you—you—touched her." The holy man's mouth was set and compressed.

"Oh, are you still carrying that young lady?" the first monk responded, a twinkle in his eye. "I put her down an hour ago."

The stress management tip illustrated by this story is very clear. Simply let go. When you think and worry about something, you give it energy. You consciously decide to give energy to either positive thoughts or negative thoughts. One good stress power management tip is to control and monitor your thoughts carefully.

How do you handle pressure and stress? Are you the kind of person who easily becomes stressed over small issues? Pressure has a way of disorienting you, scrambling your brain patterns, and causing confusion. If you do not learn to get a handle on it the moment it appears, the results could be drastic mood swings and the development of destructive behavior patterns.

There are many kinds of pressures that you will inevitably experience. However, it is not the pressure that matters; it's what you do with it that matters. How you manage pressure is totally dependent on your perception of it. In everyday life, you are exposed to many references to pressure—for example, atmospheric conditions such as high pressure or low pressure, psychological conditions such as feeling under pressure, and medical conditions such as sinus or blood pressure. Most people in our culture have felt financial pressure, peer pressure, business pressure, or marital pressure, just to name a few. Unlike atmospheric or sinus pressure, these are actually mental pressures that engender anxiety.

How do you respond when you feel as though you are under pressure? Do you thrive or deteriorate? Are you calm or do you become agitated? Just for a moment, take a candid introspection of your own history of feelings, thoughts, and motives, and don't turn away from them, even if it hurts. Building a better future depends on your ability to release and eradicate the past. You have to be willing to acknowledge things from your past, to not accept them as your present reality. In the end, a successful life will mean that you learned and grew spiritually from whatever happened.

Pressure and stress are unavoidable aspects of the world we live in. Therefore, it is absolutely vital that you constantly assess your personal thresholds in order to make mental adjustments when confronted with new challenges. The ability to cope with pressure and stress is essential in almost all walks of life, whether you're working at the checkout at a local store or as the CEO of a major corporation. This ability to cope—or the lack thereof—will be the difference between becoming focused to deal with the stress and folding under it.

Often the biggest problem is that people are oblivious to stress and where it can come from. Although stress is inevitable, it seems to have permission to come and go in people's lives as it pleases. Stress is a psychological hypothesis that only gains strength when you don't realize that you have created it. If you can create your own stresses, you can also free yourself of them. As Ralph Waldo Emerson said, "What lies behind us and what lies before us are tiny matters compared to what lies within us." Perception is supreme; how you see a matter is how it is and dictates how you will respond to it. Here are five great, easy ideas for disarming your stress by relieving you of your pressure.

1. Remember Who Is in Control: You

You have the power within you to cancel out and discharge all thoughts of negativity from your past or present. The truth is that if you refuse to take 100 percent responsibility for your life, you will not be able to change it. The world of material form simply reflects what is going on in your thinking. Don't look at the circumstances as encompassing you with no way out—view them as challenges that you are capable of overcoming.

2. Facilitate Your Time

The greatest waste in the history of mankind does not involve money, but rather time. When you don't manage your time, you are actually mismanaging your life. Every day a direct deposit of 86,400 seconds is deposited into your life account, with which you can make wise decisions. Your entire day is in your hands. People who don't respect their time will not respect yours either. Don't let time stealers rip you off, leaving you with late evenings and unaccomplished goals. Time is your most precious commodity. Use it wisely, and you can cut your pressure by as much as 90 percent.

3. Don't Rush

Whatever your desire is, don't concern yourself with physically possessing it until you have made concessions for first mentally conceiving it. You cannot possess in your life what you cannot retain in your mind. Too often people are inundated with keeping up with the Joneses . . . trying to have the latest technological device, the best office ranking, or the name-brand handbag . . . and for what? If you are in a hurry to achieve something or to get your hands on something, you will simply end up with worries. You will always be at the effect end of whatever the cause was that was programmed into your mental system. If you change what you think or do at the level of cause, you will experience a new effect. Live your life similar to how you walk, taking one step at a time. Success isn't going anywhere soon; it will be there when you get there.

4. Focus on the Solution, Not the Problem
Focus is nothing more than anxiety in reverse. Similarly, fretting about your finances will do nothing but get you worked up and mentally bent out of shape. Anxiety will usually prevent you from taking action because you are fixated on the problem, not the solution. Focus on what you want, not on what you don't want. This small shift in your psyche—from worrying about the problem to focusing on the solution—can help you adjust your response away from stress.

Get a mentor, and not just anybody. Even a focused person can be moving in the wrong direction. If you want the best for your life, get the best for your life. For example, if you are interested in really losing weight, and you choose a friend as an advisor who is in just a tad bit better shape than you are, you will not do as well as you may expect. Employ the person who is thirty to forty pounds lighter, with an ongoing record of managing diet and exercise. Learn to listen by adhering to their suggestions on how you can manhandle perplexing situations that may arise to derail your efforts to perform at your peak levels.

Focus big, not small. Sometimes, the big things we are capable of aren't obvious because our thoughts are too small. Every situation you create is small compared to every solution you can produce. Don't sweat the small stuff!

5. Stop the Mental Rehearsals

Several years ago, on one of my properties, I had a balloon payment due. I would have liked to have paid it off, but I didn't have as much liquidity at the time. My mind wanted to panic, but my heart was saying not to. That voice inside my head was saying I'd never get it done.

I'm sure you have been in this place before; fighting every negative thought . . . working diligently to end the rehearsal of a financial disaster. As soon as I settled down both mentally and physically, I cleared my mind, and my creative juices once again began to flow, as if a faucet had been turned on. My accountant and CPA were able to find money to add to the bottom line, and I was able to impress the VP who came to look at my property. I had more than I initially thought. I would have probably never known my possibilities if I had given in to the panic.

Don't stress over things you can easily correct. When troubles and circumstances are trying to entertain you, don't pay the price and give them an audience. Believe me, they are not worth the admission price—their act is lousy.

Rethink what you believe, rethink focus, and rethink possible!

CHAPTER FOURTEEN

Don't Suppress What You Possess

"People of talent resemble a musical instrument more closely than they do a musician. Without outside help, they produce not a single sound, but given even the slightest touch, and a magnificent tune emanates from them."
—Franz Grillparzer

Just because you can't see it doesn't mean you don't have it.

Once there was a farmer who was very hard working. He had developed a vineyard that gave a rich crop of grapes every year. Unluckily, his sons were very easygoing young men. They seldom cared to help their father in his work, and the farmer was often worried about their future.

Reaching a ripe old age, the farmer fell ill. It looked as if his end was near. So he called his sons and said to them, "Dear sons! My days are numbered. Before dying, I want to tell you that in my

Turn on Your Life

grapery lies a hidden treasure. Dig it out after my death." Saying so, the old farmer died.

After performing last rites for their father, the sons began digging the vineyard. They dug every inch of it but found nothing.

But the digging led to a rich crop as had never before been seen, even in their father's lifetime. So, the sons came to know what their father meant by the hidden treasure: they had learned that hard work is the key to a gold mine.

Now is the time for you to express all of the hidden qualities you may be involuntarily repressing because of your inability to get past the personal struggles and battles from your past. People are inundated with constant thoughts of the past—of what they may have been denied while growing up, or of the physical abuse they may have experienced, or of the hurtful words they may have been told by people they loved and respected. Dr. Benjamin Carson was one of those individuals told that he was slow and had an inability to learn anything. However, these labels did not stick!

One day, I was listening to a speech by Dr. Carson, who recently retired as Director of Pediatric Neurosurgery at Johns Hopkins Hospital; he said something that caught my attention. When he was a young boy, whenever he had a problem, he was always apprehensive about going to his mother for an answer. He knew that, in response to his question, she would ask him a question, such as, "Son, do you have a brain?" He knew that when he answered with a resounding yes, she would then say, "Well, go figure it out!" This was the beginning of his quest for knowledge and his pursuit of wisdom.

People often ask God for things He has already given them. Their challenge only exists because what they have isn't immediately identifiable or they are looking for something other than the thing He wove into the fabric of their being.

Every person wants to succeed in having a better life and fulfilling his or her lifelong dream. I want to help make this happen for you, but I cannot do it without you. I am locked into one of the most precarious situations; I want to do so much for others, but I'm often confronted by individuals stuck on doubt and fear. I have learned that most people don't want answers; what they want is a hand to comprehensively lead them step by step so that the weight and risk is on the other person.

There are four things people find themselves complaining about not having enough of when it comes to succeeding in life and business, and yet all four of these things, which each individual possesses in abundance, are actually either squandered or mismanaged. The problem is not that people don't have enough of these items; it's that they do a poor job of managing these items.

1. TIME

The excuse of not having enough time could not be further from the truth. Every person on this planet is allotted 86,400 seconds a day. Think of it as $86,400 deposited into your bank account. This gives you $31,536,000 (seconds) a year deposited into your life account.

You have more than enough dollars (time) to employ a personal trainer to help you develop a six-pack, to employ the best writers to help you write a bestseller, to attend wealth seminars to help you become rich and to better manage your money, or anything else you really want to achieve. When you learn how to manage your time, you are also learning how to manage your life. This in turn helps you manage your money. Properly managing your money helps you manage your lifestyle, because time really is money. Time is your most precious commodity; it gives you a head start and puts you at an advantage. When it comes to succeeding in life or business, you have more than enough time to make your world the best place on the planet. This is not to say that you have all the time in the world, just ample time.

You can exchange your time to make all the money you desire. However, you cannot trade in your money to make more time. So the next time you claim to not have enough time to accomplish your task, think of all the money you are throwing away. When you schedule your time, you are actually investing your time and using it wisely.

2. MONEY

To develop and cleverly maintain your life and your own business for maximum profit is unequivocally the best way to wealth. There is a misleading notion that you need more than enough money and the most meticulous business plan in order to successfully launch a business. I want to confront and meet head-on this frame of mind and prove that this is not how it has to be. It doesn't mean that I am negating the importance of money in starting a business. I only want to demonstrate that money is often an illusion when it comes to starting a business. What is more important is that you exercise perseverance, enthusiasm, and commitment because you most likely will experience failure a few times before you experience success.

Rather than the case being that you need more money, the truth of the matter is that you either need to change your perception of what monies you have or you need to learn how to use the money you have. It's like playing basketball and learning how to

Don't Suppress What You Possess

move without the ball so that you can position yourself for a better shot when you receive the ball. If you think the amount of money you presently have is not enough, then what you need is to unleash your creative juices and find out how to do what you want with the money in your possession.

In some cases, money may be the seed to money, but oftentimes money is created from ideas and concepts. There's no limit to the number of ideas we can have. Instead of thinking that you don't have enough, start to imagine and believe that you have an ample supply of money. Your mind will stretch and scan every possible avenue to discover what you knew existed all along.

One business venture I put together, a restaurant, is on one of the US military installations. Once I got through the government red tape and signed the contract, the next thing I was to do was work out a plan of how to build out my suite with hardly any cash. I had property that I could have converted into cash, but that would take some time to do. Literally, I didn't have enough cash, but I had a lot of ideas. When you don't have all the money you need for a project, your ideas can manufacture the resources to make your task possible.

I needed a contractor to build out the suite, so I immediately created one, along with one of my employees. By cutting out the contractor and being one myself, I could divert profits toward my project. Next, I needed subcontractors to build out my job for about two hundred and eighty thousand, in which the cost did not include all the equipment. Liquidity is powerful, but the expectation of cash is even more powerful.

An idea came to me at about three o'clock in the morning. I called my foreman and contract negotiator to inform each subcontractor that, because this job was on government property, they would have to qualify and fund their portion of the job within 90 to 120 days after completion. I agreed with some of the subs that I would do them a favor and pay them 10 to 25 percent to help them out. This would show good faith on my part, but in actuality, it was a tactic to give the subcontractors a sense of confidence in my ability to pay.

I knew that the tenet improvement amount from the landlord would give me about sixty to seventy thousand after I received a certificate of occupancy. With this amount deposited into my account, I would be able to use that money to pay off some of the subcontractors. With the grand opening and sales initially up at the opening of my restaurant, I would have every need taken care of by the time 90 to 120 days rolled around. It all happened according to the plan based on the dream I had.

So, you tell me. What did I need most—money or ingenuity? Learning how to be resourceful is vital, especially when you need resources to live your dream. You personally possess more stimulating thoughts than you could possibly put down on paper. Dive into your personal vast ocean of ideas and start swimming. Solution is the best resolution.

3. Connections

Everyone has them and everyone needs them. Being appropriately connected means a lot in our society. It means everything in nature—it's a web of life. Species and populations in isolation accomplish little. It's only when they are linked that things begin to happen and ecosystems within the framework of life and business begin to work and thrive. Generally, the more diverse things are, the more links there are and the better things function.

The right connection can be the bridge to your success, and the wrong connection can be the downward escalator to your demise. Despite which is chosen, the outcome is predetermined by your connection. The right mentor knows how to not compete with you;

the wrong mentor will block your view of your strengths to make him or herself seem larger than life to you.

Connecting is important because, without it, there is no flow of an inheritance of knowledge and experience. Oprah has said, "For every one of us that succeeds, it is because there's somebody there to show you the way out." Your future is shot if you have no link to anyone's past accomplishments. Someone has to pave the road and lay the foundation to where you are going—or be the example of how to get there—so you can reach your goal.

Advisors are everywhere. However, you need to pursue the mentor who is qualified, not just available. Good mentors are not always available just so you can talk; you need a psychiatrist for that. Yet mentors who understand their roles are usually present when something needs to be taught.

This is where most people have trouble. They have been so programmed by society to believe in the "get rich quick" schemes and the "instant gratification" fixes that they claim to neither have the time, nor patience, nor understanding for the things that may require consistent action for many years. Connecting yourself with the right people will make all the difference in the world when it comes to thriving instead of surviving.

There is no shortage of qualified connections; simply choosing the right connection for you is all you need. You must recognize greatness when you are in the presence of it. It will not always demand attention. Jesus went many places where He was undetected and unrecognized. The presence of great leaders can be unassuming, but when you listen to their words, you will know that their knowledge is crowned with wisdom.

You may have to find your connections in the most unlikely places while doing some of the most uncomfortable things. You see, mentors don't need you; but you obviously need them. Electricity doesn't need you—you need electricity. When you plug your appliances into a wall socket, what you are doing is tapping into the power that can make your appliances work for you. If you want a slice of bread, all you need to do is go to the store and buy a loaf of bread and eat it. But, if you would like a slice of toast, then power is what you need after you get the loaf of bread. The power is waiting for you to connect to help you get where you desire to be in life.

4. Knowledge and Wisdom
Knowledge
Knowledge is needed for any business venture or simply to make it through life successfully. It is critical that you pursue knowledge. However, what you should pursue is the knowledge of someone who knows how to do what you want done.

Just like a seed, you have everything you need inside of you to succeed; you just need to be planted in the right soil and cultivated. What you may not possess, someone else does. For instance, you may not be a plumber, but you can call a plumber with more experience who knows exactly how to solve your problem. You might be the kind of person who demonstrates your knowledge about repairing older model cars, but you may own a brand new S Class Mercedes Benz, which you need to take to a certified Mercedes Benz mechanic for repairs.

Seeking knowledge should be a never-ending pursuit because your current knowledge may not be adequate for your next level in life. And yet, knowledge does not work on its own.

Wisdom
As important as knowledge is, it is not nearly as important as wisdom. In fact, wisdom can use knowledge, but knowledge cannot

use wisdom. Those who believe that knowledge is just as important as wisdom usually like to collect information—which may make a person smarter but not necessarily wiser. To know something is just like knowing nothing if you can't apply what you know.

I believe what most people have accomplished in life is only a tiny portion of their potential; most accomplishments come from pursuing what is manageable without really having to exert energy beyond their comfort zone. Imagine having the power to change the world, yet only thinking about changing your furniture around. Commit yourself to doing something *BIGGER* than yourself. Throw your heart and mind over the banister of limitations, and your body will follow. It is not the lack of knowledge that is destroying your chances at a better life. It is doing nothing with the knowledge you have.

People who negotiate for increased wages believe they earn it by working harder on their job. On the other hand, I believe that the secret to pay increases is not working harder on your job, but rather working harder on yourself.

Those who walk according to fear always do what they know they can do. Those who walk according to faith do what they believe they can do without having ever done it before. There is a difference between making a mistake and being one. Wisdom will help you make the best decisions with your present knowledge for your life.

There are no excuses; everyone has the ability to succeed. Get started today! Time, money, connections, knowledge, and wisdom are all compacted in your spirit, body, and mind. There are no shortages of these qualities; there is just a lack of hunger to feed

Turn on Your Life

on these until they consume you to live a better life. Find them and make the best use of them, and they will produce dividends that will bring you great wealth.

You would be surprised about what the Bible has stored inside you. God is too faithful for you to ask for something big and only believe for something small. God wrapped Himself in a baby called Jesus and changed the world forever. You are designed by divine to do the same.

CHAPTER FIFTEEN

DON'T WAIT FOR THE CHANCE OF A LIFETIME

"When written in Chinese, the word 'crisis' is composed of two characters. One represents danger and the other represents opportunity."
—JOHN F. KENNEDY

Waiting is something I hate to do; while I am waiting for something, I can only imagine how many opportunities have passed by.

I REMEMBER WHEN MY FIRST-BORN SON was learning how to play baseball. I could tell that he wasn't interested in playing, but he joined the team nevertheless. He played left field and was a little intimidated about the ball coming in his direction . . . okay—he was scared of the ball. I would often say, "Son, don't be afraid of the ball; you can catch it when it comes to you."

During one game, the batter went to the batter box. My son kept yelling, "Batter, batter, batter . . . batter." The pitcher rounded up and threw the perfect ball, and the batter hit the ball out to left field. I thought, "Here comes the ball! Get it!" Instead, my son stood still and the ball passed by about seven feet away from him.

"Son, why didn't you get the ball?" I asked him.

"It didn't come to me!" he replied

"All you had to do is move a little to your right and you could have had the ball. You've got to move because the ball usually will not come directly to you."

Needless to say, we lost the game, and my son went on to play football.

Opportunities rarely come to those who sit on their couch watching soap operas. In fact, sitting in your living room waiting for a hand to come out of heaven with a million dollars is just as useless as sitting around waiting for a leopard to change its spots or a tiger its stripes.

One old cliché says, "Good things come to those who wait." I say that good things are the leftovers from people who got the best things because they decided not to wait. The great comedian Jonathan Winters once said, "I couldn't wait for success, so I went on without it." People will not always recognize your talent, but they will give voice to your persistence.

Are you sitting and waiting for someone or something extraordinary to happen for you? Have you been sitting back in hopes that God would somehow touch someone's heart to give you enough money to start your business? Have you thought about the opportunities you miss on a daily basis while waiting for your miracle? Let's face it; opportunities are more frequent than miracles. I am not belittling or dismissing the reality of miracles. I am merely stating the truth when it comes to a person who is in a position to make something positive happen for him or herself. People who wait for their ship to arrive at the dock are usually the ones who are always missing the boat.

Consider this reality about those whose lives are in a holding pattern, who are waiting for a chance to decide when to make their move. These people have high hopes based on a wish that things will soon turn in their favor, which is only an indication that they actually lack inspiration. Opportunities are all around you, but they are difficult to see when your concept of an opportunity is more like a handout.

Take my advice and seek ways to ignite and unleash your inspiration. Remind yourself of what truly matters and who is important to you. Think of what inspires you. Start looking for inspiration in the most unlikely places. In fact, look for inspiration everywhere—in movies, books, TV shows, and people you encounter daily. Listen to the conversation of children as they converse with one another, because they can stimulate and strike a chord causing your mind to return to times when life was fun and exciting.

Some of the most highly paid people in the nation are in the business of inspiring others. Many of these wealthy people have claimed to receive their inspiration from doing for others what someone did for them. For instance, Oprah Winfrey inspires millions while she herself is inspired by the people her foundation has helped. She is known as the greatest female philanthropist in the United States because she believes in people—and in making a difference in the lives of those she has been able to touch. I believe that she is blessed because she is such a giver to the cause of humanity, and therefore, her mind is constantly open to more ideas to increase her billionaire status.

Inspiration has always come from giving and so does opportunity. Sir John Templeton asked himself this question: "Is it my philosophy that what I am given—in terms of my abilities, my intelligence, and my material success—should be returned to the world in some form that will help others?" If you can pose this same question to yourself and answer with a resounding yes, you are already a giver and your life is enriched.

Keep in mind that spiritual progress and material success are closely connected. Never be afraid to give to others or charitable causes. Serve others and you serve yourself. If you are intimidated about giving in general and cannot see the benefit in it, you will lock yourself out of opportunities and become completely blind to the ones that are right in front of your face.

You can live an incredibly wealthy life, if you can believe that you can live an incredibly wealthy life. Unfortunately, most people believe just the opposite. These people struggle with increasing their wealth, but they have no problem with increasing their debt. They are disgruntled, discouraged, and often depressed about everything in their world. However, it does not have to be this way.

Incomes of people have changed just because they started thinking differently and speaking differently. My friend, that is all that is needed—an attitude adjustment. If you look up, there is no limit, but if you look down, you are standing on it.

Are you looking for opportunities, or are you waiting on one? Opportunities always look bigger going, but appear smaller coming. Your big opportunity may be right where you are. Sometimes, opportunities are missed because we don't know what we're looking for. It is said that Alexander the Great was asked by one of his captains in his army, "Would you take the next city if you had the opportunity to do so?" to which Alexander the Great replied, "Opportunity? Why, I don't wait for opportunities; I create opportunities." It can be very costly for you to feel as if you have all the time in the world to recline in your easy chair waiting for that opportunity to present itself. As you wait, options become limited and your ability to recognize opportunities becomes nebulous.

THE BANK OF IDEAS

There are many people who have a bank full of ideas, and they continue to deposit new ideas into this bank until they decide when it is the right moment to do something with them. Some of these ideas can actually be great ones. Yet they are never withdrawn and just sit in this bank due to people's beliefs in a lack of provisions to make them happen.

One young man partially shared what I thought was a great concept. However, he was afraid that someone would steal his idea and he would be penniless from his own creation. I said, "Well, think of it this way; as long as you have your idea stored away, no one will ever be able to get their hands on it and benefit from it, and you will still be penniless. But if you withdraw your wonderful concept and invest the pennies you have to make a prototype of it, you can present it to a couple of viable companies that assist inventors, and you can eventually have billions of pennies."

Fraser Doherty, at the age of just fourteen, started making jams from his grandmother's recipes in Edinburgh, Scotland. Originally, his customer base was limited to neighbors and friends from his church, but business picked up quickly, and by age sixteen, he left school to work on his jams full time. Doherty started renting out a factory a few days each month, and today, over two thousand stores sell Doherty's SuperJam. He's in his thirties. He didn't wait to get an education—and it paid off. Now his net worth is about $6 million. Truly, Fraser's story is a recipe for success.

While I do not advocate dropping out of school, this story is a clear example that, when a "should" turns into a "must," success is inevitable.

CHAPTER SIXTEEN

Embrace Your Future

"Let others lead small lives, but not you. Let others argue over small things, but not you. Let others cry over small hurts, but not you. Let others leave their future in someone else's hands, but not you."
—Jim Rohn

Release your past and recognize the potential of the present moment. Embrace your future and unleash your power to create a better tomorrow.

A HUNGRY WOLF was going over a highway one evening. He met a dog. The dog was fat and appeared happy. The wolf made friends with the dog.

"You are looking better. It appears you are happy and enjoying life. Your skin is so nice. You have been fed properly with vitamins, proteins, and minerals," said the wolf.

"Look, my friend, my life is simple," the dog responded. "I watch my master's house. He feeds me four times a day. I have been given a small house where I sleep well. I don't have any difficulties."

"Then your life is good. I also wish the same. But you see my plight. I am always hungry. You see my bones. I am fed very little. I don't have vitamins and proteins in my food."

"OK, then, come with me. Live with me. You will also be happy. Luxury makes a person," said the dog. The wolf agreed. Both of them reached the house where the dog lived. Both were happy.

As the wolf entered the house, he happened to see the top of the dog's neck. He found no hairs there. "Why are there no hairs on your neck?" the wolf asked the dog.

"Oh! My dear friend. Why do you ask? My master puts a belt on my neck. The belt rubs my neck while it's tied tightly to a chain. My master pulls it and pushes me into the kennel," said the dog.

"What? Collar and chain?" the wolf said and didn't enter further. He was astonished to hear what the dog had said. "Friend, let me go back. I am not jealous of you. You eat good food. But you are tied here. My bones are thin, true. But I am free in my world. I can go anywhere I like. Thank you. I shall go back."

And the wolf went back to his forest.

In a time unprecedented, knowledge currently doubles every two years. With the increase of knowledge comes an increase in problems as well. Still, the increase of knowledge is not able to remain current with the increase of problems. Information, facts, and data are the knowledge you have that are a result of your past experiences, and so are they the source of your problems. No matter what you have come to believe about your past, your past does have a grip on you—but you also have a grip on your past. Yet people often move forward in life with their past experiences instead of with their future hopes.

Many things that are a constant bother to you will no longer be as soon as you make up your mind that you are done with them. The pain and disappointments of your past have a tendency to hang around because you subconsciously see them as acquaintances. They will leave you when you decide that you no longer have any use for them.

The most dangerous thing you can do to your future is to never let go of your past. The second most dangerous thing you can do is to live your life and discover at the end that you never really lived at all. If you continue to focus on the pain and failure of your past, you will never truly experience the joy of your future.

Looking back can cause your future to appear hopeless, as though your best years have already passed. Often women in their forties and fifties, especially those who are divorced or widowed, have all but given up on the possibilities of finding another spouse or living the rest of their life with a sense of purpose. Some women have concluded that being "boy-less" increases their chances of being joyless. However, this is far from the truth.

I believe that looking back would not be so harmful if people did not see the past as the good old days. If those were the good old days, then the future has to have better days. When life brings us struggle or hard moments, it is easy to hold onto those fortunate times and to carry our past forward with us. This is unhealthy and harmful. These thoughts of our past hold us hostage in a world of fantasy. In other words, we accept these former days as the best of times and give up the prospects of a better future.

I want to make something very clear to you before you sentence the rest of your life to the consistency of the mundane. Human beings are powerful and wonderful creatures of great possibilities, and the sooner you believe this down to the crevasses of your being, the more of these possibilities you will experience. People are meant to live in a state of perpetual newness, not weighed down by their pasts or things they are holding onto. In order to release what is old and unproductive, you need to believe you are done with it. That feeling, the heaviness in life, is you carrying something with you that you no longer need.

Most people live their lives based on logic instead of living their lives based on faith. So, when something occurs in their lives, they try to figure out why. And this, my friend, can drive you crazy! Logic makes no sense to faith, but logic with its foundation in faith works out every time. A person of faith and courage says forget about it, it is in the past, move forward.

What makes the impossible possible? What turns problems into solutions? What causes the invisible to become visible? What actually happens when you are faced with a problem? Do you run from it or are you inherently mentally focused on how you can solve it?

The things that matter the most must never be at the mercy of the things that matter the least. The Apostle Paul of the Bible, who is in my opinion one of the greatest Bible characters, experienced a great deal of adversity and yet remained focused; he discovered the secret to moving on: "This one thing I do: forgetting those things which are behind, and reaching forth unto those things which are before" (Philippians 3:13). Why be concerned about a tainted past when your future is spotless?

STARTING OVER
Sometimes the hardest part isn't learning how to let go but rather learning how to start over. You are not starting over new when you are starting over doing the same old things. Everyone can

benefit from a release of their pasts. In fact, this release is vital for growth and change. Otherwise, people are living in the past and just waiting for the future to end.

When you release your past—an event, an old issue, a person—you are releasing yourself into your future; you are allowing yourself to be who God says you are, not who you think you are. Releasing your past is a must for evolving, which in turn is necessary for facing new challenges. Whenever you are stuck in the old reality—whether in sickness or financial woes or just unhappiness—it is all based in memories of past fears that you can't seem to shake off.

One of the principles I've learned about releasing your past is that you cannot purposefully let go of the past without first facing it. You have to look at your past and command it! When you do this, one thing that will become apparent to you is that you may be afraid of success more than you are of failure. Fear of success may sound strange to you—who wouldn't want to be successful? But experiencing success may be unchartered territory, while the familiarity of failures and disappointments aligns more with your comfort zone.

When you are determined to embrace your future, to reach out for it with all you have within you, it is inevitable that you will experience success. How much success you experience is totally dependent on your desire to do what is necessary to accomplish it. Success can be scary for some because it involves a change in environment and friends. In fact, success can be intimidating and demanding; it involves more challenges and responsibilities—and that can be threatening.

One time I counseled with a couple who had a problem losing the additional pounds they both had put on over the course of their marriage. She wanted to lose weight, but he was adamant that it wasn't necessary, and he would subconsciously sabotage her success. She couldn't figure out why he would promise that both of them would get on a regiment and work out to lose weight but always find reasons to start at another time. He really loved his wife, and she loved him equally. In my communication with them, I asked a question about his past, about his relationship with his parents.

After he spent several moments evading my question, I figured there was something in his past that caused a great deal of trepidation. He had an issue with insecurity. As a child, his parents got divorced because his mother had an extramarital affair. After the divorce, he went to live with his father, but his mother went to live with her lover. Over the years, he saw his father deteriorate, becoming an introvert and experiencing problems trusting people.

"Don't you want you and your wife to live a healthy life? Does it bother you that your wife is unhappy with herself and battling a low self-esteem?" I asked the husband.

"I want her to be happy." He put his head down and sighed.

I asked the question that I knew he didn't want to answer because it would bring up harbored feelings and cause him to face his apprehensions. "Are you afraid if your wife loses weight that she will become attractive to other men and perhaps have an affair and leave you?"

This one major question was the key to opening the floodgates. The husband's emotions began to pour out like a faucet turned on full force. He voiced a great deal of resentment toward his mother for cheating on his dad. He watched his father give up on life. His father's health deteriorated, and he died a lonely man. He just didn't want that to happen with his wife. His way of ensuring that this would never occur was to remain overweight.

The husband in this story had an important decision to make, and the wrong decision could have had dire consequences for both him and his marriage. His wife was not the problem. In fact, he was not the problem—his past was. This man allowed his past to continue to interrupt any success for the present and the future.

What can fear of being successful with your life lead to? Fear of success can without a doubt induce self-destructive behavior. In the process, you become questionable to others and to yourself as well. As a result, you become less motivated, and your life without an ambition leads you toward incessant underachievement and failures. Letting go of the past doesn't mean forgetting it; it means knowing that you cannot change it. Let it go! Embrace your future.

Don't feel helpless, as if you are at the mercy of random occurrences. There are four essential steps you can take to keep your spirits high, no matter how challenging and discouraging a situation is. Mark this moment as a power moment for your life! You are in control, not out of control. Love your life; don't hate it. This is the only life you have—why live it with regrets and depression when you can turn on your life light and be happy, fulfilled, and content? Nothing and no one is stopping you from experiencing your own revolution. Go for the gusto, and together, we will help you walk this journey of embracing your future.

1. CHOOSE TO BE HAPPY

Happiness is not difficult to achieve. Happiness is a state of mind, not the state of a situation. Your situations have just as much of a chance to change as does your mind. Change your mind, and you change your state. It is almost impossible for you to visualize yourself as a happy and content person, and not *be* happy and content. A circumstance doesn't make you happy or sad; it is your perspective of your circumstances that affects your perception that leads you to either react with sadness or respond with happiness. Happiness is humanity's original state, while sadness is a forced emotion. No person lives in misery involuntarily.

2. NOW (No Opportunity Wasted) Is Your Power Moment

You cannot rewrite your past, but you can illustrate your future by drawing it out in your present moment. Your future is one big blank sheet of paper (days) that needs your present activity to sketch out what you want it to look like. God may hold tomorrow in His hands, but what happens in it is clearly up to you.

3. Don't Be Modest About What You Want

A false sense of modesty keeps your abilities and true desires locked in a cage of despair. Most people are aware of what they want in life—it's just that many who do know are too modest to say it, in fear that it may show up those who feel as though they do not deserve much. I may not want a twenty-thousand-square-foot home, but the home I have is what I truly want. And my home doesn't speak modesty compared to most homes. Warren Buffett may live in a modest home and drive a modest car, but there is nothing modest about his wealth.

One of my protégés was speaking to me about his life and future. He mentioned how his desire was not about money and things. I said, "It will be about money when you get hungry." Money, clothes, food, transportation, furniture, etc., are all-too-important needs that should never be undermined as trivial. It is not that we place our major attention on material things rather than spiritual things, but it helps that when you are hungry you can buy food, and when you are cold you can purchase the proper clothing, and when you need to provide for your family you have the resources to do so. This, my friend, needs no apology.

4. Destroy Your Wish List

A wish list is a thought list of things you really don't believe that you can achieve or have in life. Destroy your wish list, and write down your list of goals. A wish is a fantasy; but a goal is a realistic target for which you can develop a process to achieve.

To have success in life, goals are essential. They are what you are aiming for to ultimately achieve your dream vision. If you have not written down any goals as of yet, I would encourage you to do so. Under each goal item, place up to five things you can do to help you achieve your goals. Remember, it is not good to have goals without developing a system to achieve them.

If you want to excel in life, to tap into your God-given potential, self-motivation is essential. You must know how to motivate yourself. You don't need other people to push you to do something you like. You don't need other people to tell you to go and do what must be done. In fact, you must take the initiative to work on your own. Getting started is the most difficult part in many cases, especially when resources are few and your energy level is low.

Motivation is the drive to persevere, because on the road to success there is never a crowd on the extra mile! You should thank God even for the little resources you do have. He has given you the "seed" that will grow into the "forest" you desire.

CHAPTER SEVENTEEN
Explore Your Possibilities

"The only limits to the possibilities in your life
tomorrow are the buts you use today."
—Les Brown

Possibilities are all around you; you just have to rethink possible.

Noah was five hundred years old when God told him to build an ark. Noah had to come to grips with his mortality, only to realize that age was not a reason to quit while he was still living.

There is an old maxim that says, "Don't wait for your ship to come to shore; build one." Noah did not build an ark for God; he built an ark for him, his family, and anyone who adhered to his warning. However, like most geniuses who live in a world of possibilities, he found himself ridiculed and laughed at until he accomplished what he talked about doing. God gave Noah the objective to build an ark, but Noah had to mastermind the strategy and techniques in order to build it. Just imagine the intelligence and creativeness of Noah to build such a device without having any prior example laid before him. Did he ever consider the enormous magnitude of undertaking such a task?

❧

Satchel Paige was the oldest "rookie" ever to play Major League Baseball when he was signed by the Cleveland Indians in 1948. However, his exact age was not known with certainty. Satchel Paige was once asked by a sports reporter of his age compared to the much younger players he was playing against. His reply was, "If you didn't know the year you were born, how old would you be?"

❧

The most powerful thing a person can ever build is a healthy self-image. The next most powerful thing a person can do is to destroy one's own self-image. Each tree in the forest grows from a single seed; but one spark can destroy the entire forest.

The key to improving your life and enjoying it can only be found after you have initially become truly acquainted with who you are. Personal growth begins at the point of personal awareness. It is at this point that you will realize you are who you are and not who you act like. Too often people try to reinvent who they are when they haven't a clue who they are to begin with.

Have you ever heard someone say after going through a negative experience, "I don't know who I am anymore"? If all it takes is going through adverse circumstances for people to lose their identity, it might suggest that they were not certain of who they were in the first place. I often say that once you discover who you are from a God perspective, don't change you; just change how you do you! Stop being your own worst enemy.

If we are to learn anything from God, it would be that life is supposed to work. Yet for the staggering seven billion people on this planet, life is not about thriving—it is about surviving, just trying to hang on. Is this really the best that can be expected?

Have people simply been given life so that many of them can become an enemy to life itself? Are they literally killing their future prospects of living a full life because they refuse to accept the reality that their norm is nothing but a façade? Are they trapped in a snare that they have set for themselves or that someone else has set for them? Regardless of who set the trap, most people do not realize that they are incarcerated and restricted spiritually, physically, and mentally by their own beliefs.

What happens when an immovable object clashes with an unstoppable force? Imagine a speeding, out-of-control train coming into a station with no hope of stopping and all efforts to change its course unsuccessful. A catastrophe is going to occur, and destruction is going to be the result. The same thing happens when it comes to truth versus tradition. This is not to suggest that all traditions collide with truth. Traditions that are aligned with truth are just as wonderful as truth itself. However, traditions become problematic when they clash with the truth.

So, what are traditions? Traditions are habits, customs, or practices that you have believed and practiced all your life. Often with traditions, change is like trying to crack a safe with billions of dollars inside, but with no clue what the combination is. In life, the combination to unlock all your possibilities is not in numbers; your combination is in what you believe.

NOT A MISTAKE, MERELY MISTAKEN

Could it be that you have been blinded to your brilliance, kept in the dark about your strength, kept ignorant of your power and magnificence? The matrix that exists around you is a counterfeit world that has people in it just like you who are convinced of their limitations and persuaded that other people who experience success in life are touched with special powers. This belief becomes an excuse for not doing what is in their hearts. No one stops them from being a success. No one can keep them from accomplishing their goals but themselves. They are their own worst enemy, and they are their own greatest asset—the same is true for you.

Living an unproductive life and struggling with unimaginable mental challenges is not really living at all. The fear of challenge can easily be conquered by simply starting your dream instead of continuously talking about it.

If you are going to disconnect from this maze of limited possibilities and demonstrate the ability to stand up to the challenge of doing anything and everything you set your mind and heart to do, you will have to make a firm, definite decision. Life is about you accomplishing things, not sitting back and watching others do what you are capable of doing.

Why focus on how big the task at hand is when you can focus on how big the ability God placed in you actually is? You are more than capable of accomplishing so much more than what you have accomplished up to this point. The chapters of your life are still being written, even as you read this book.

I have doctor friends who tell me that they often say to some of their overweight patients, "You have to watch your weight and what you are eating because you are overweight and borderline diabetic." Patients hear the warning time and time again and think that they can turn it around anytime they want. When they arrive for their next doctor's visit, their vital signs are read and they get on the weight scale and things are even worse than they were at their previous visit.

Like most people, they say after a revelation such as this, "How did I put on all this weight?" The real question is how could they expect anything different when they did not change their behavior?

Usually, when people waste opportunities, they leave it to someone else to clean up. My suggestion to the many people who dare not look inside themselves is to not be afraid—look inside and see all the great potential waiting to be used. Don't count all the things you feel that you can't do; count the things you can do. And, as you focus on the things you can accomplish, you will begin to exert yourself to do things that you've only imagined you could achieve.

Don't use failure or misfortune as an excuse to not reconsider your possibilities. In order to get back on your feet, you have to get off your butt. Go ahead, stand up! There is more to you than what you first believed. What does not seem to be apparent will become clear as you discover and use those talents and gifts that were buried under the debris of doubt and fear.

Do not compare yourself with others; you are your own competition. You have to beat your previous personal best . . . and believe me, you will surpass it. You will reach higher, dig deeper, run faster, fight harder, prepare better, and imagine even greater things, all because you simply did everything you could and you left nothing to chance.

CHAPTER EIGHTEEN
GET THE GOLD

"Formal education will make you a living; self-education will make you a fortune."
—JIM ROHN

If you are doing what you love and it is making you a decent living, but you are also doing something on the side and it is making you a fortune—drop what you love and put your heart into what you're doing on the side.

JAMES WILSON MARSHALL was an American carpenter and sawmill operator whose discovery of gold in the American River in California on January 24, 1848, set the stage for the California Gold Rush. The mill property was owned by Johan Sutter, who employed Marshall to build his mill. On the morning of January 24, 1848, Marshall was examining the channel below the mill when he noticed some shiny flecks in the channel bed. As later recounted by Marshall:

I picked up one or two pieces and examined them attentively; and having some general knowledge of minerals, I could not call to mind more than two which in any way resembled this, sulphuret of iron, very bright and brittle; and gold, bright, yet malleable. I then tried it between two rocks, and found that it could be beaten into a different shape, but not broken. I then collected four or five pieces and went up to Mr. Scott (who was working at the carpenter's bench making the mill wheel) with the pieces in my hand and said, "I have found it."

"What is it?" inquired Scott.

"Gold," I answered.

"Oh! No," replied Scott, "That can't be."

I said, "I know it to be nothing else."

Marshall shared his discovery with Sutter, who performed further tests on the gold and told Marshall that it was "of the finest quality, of at least twenty-three karat, which was 96 percent pure." The metal was also confirmed to be gold after members of Marshall's crew performed tests on the metal—boiling it in a lye solution and hammering it to test its malleability. Marshall, still primarily concerned with the completion of the sawmill, permitted his crew to search for gold during their free time.

News of the discovery soon reached around the world. The immediate impact for Marshall was negative. His sawmill failed when all the able-bodied men in the area abandoned everything to search for gold. Before long, arriving hordes of prospectors forced him off Sutter's land, and Marshall soon left the area. By the time Marshall returned to Sutter's Fort, four days later, the war had ended and California was about to become an American possession.

The wave of gold seekers turned everyone's attention away from the mill, which eventually fell into disrepair and was never used as intended. Neither Marshall nor Sutter ever profited from the gold discovery.

People have a tendency to ignore the urgency of the moment. What could be more pressing than to respond to the clarion sound of . . . GOLD? Two things occurred that caused a misfortune instead of a fortune for the two men from the story.

1. They Did Not Stake Their Claim

What does it mean to stake a claim? The idiom comes from the early United States' history. During a gold rush or the opening of newly acquired territories, a citizen could run wooden stakes into the ground, marking land, and everything he found on that land would be legally considered his. To plainly put it, it's not your land or your property until the proof of the stakes is in the ground.

You will never benefit from something you have never owned. Ownership is staking your claim for what is now legitimately yours. Don't be like these two men who started the gold rush, yet who only ended up with the initial pieces of gold they found. They had untold riches but never claimed them.

One in four Texans has unclaimed property from forgotten bank accounts, uncashed checks, security deposits, and utility refunds. There is currently about $3 billion in property that has not been claimed and approximately $800 million in shared property that has been partially claimed and paid to some of the owners. It's never too late to make a claim, because it's your money. Some poor soul is sitting in their house complaining about not having enough money, and they have no clue that they are millionaires.

Every person in this country can go online to www.unclaimed.org, click on a state, put in their name, and see if they have any unclaimed money. I was able to collect several checks from my State Treasurer Department for money they were holding in my name. Once I staked my claim, I received a check.

It is sad for people to have lived their entire lives as paupers without discovering that they were worth millions of dollars. Think about the untold millions hiding in the crevasses of your brain, waiting to be launched by you figuring out how to get your idea out of your head and into the millions of homes in the United States and other nations.

I learned a long time ago that people don't actually have a money problem—they have a faith problem. Think about it; you are not short on money—you're short on ideas. You can have the knowledge to do something, but you lack the self-confidence to do it. Money is all around you; you just have to open your eyes and see it.

2. THEY WERE TOO PREOCCUPIED WITH THE SAWMILL

Forget the sawmill; *get the gold!* What could have been in the minds of these two men that made them believe that a facility to cut wood was more valuable than the gold? Wasn't the owner of the sawmill building his workshop to make money? Was he so prideful of his personal work that he was willing to forego millions of dollars? Mr. Sutter was distracted by his personal sawmill project and didn't realize his dream of being wealthy could have come true but by different means.

Are you missing the forest for the trees? Think about the many opportunities you may have wasted while trying to resurrect a dead project that never had the possibility of being productive. In the process, you'll end up losing the sawmill *and* the gold.

Some people are so busy working hard that working smart scares them. What is wrong with not wanting to work so hard? If there is an easier way of doing something or a shorter route to get to where you want to be, as long as it doesn't compromise your ethics, take it. I think that one of the keys to longevity in business, in order to avoid burnout, is to learn to use your time wisely, to be consistent, and to be flexible.

This principle works for marriages, raising children, and life in general. It will help you focus on the important things in life, while honing in on the major and not on the minor. Your dream perspective will be clearer, and you will understand that it's not the dream that counts—it's what the dream does and who you become in the process.

CHAPTER NINETEEN

GET WHAT LIFE IS HOLDING FOR YOU

"In the beginning there was nothing and God said 'Let there be light,' and there was still nothing but everybody could see it."
—Dave Thomas

Money is not the root of all evil—the love of money is. Therefore, you can have all the money you don't love.

THERE IS A STORY that was told to me years ago when I was going through one of the roughest periods of my life. My financial situation was at its lowest, my family was torn apart, and to add insult to injury, I was the gossip of the town. However, this story helped me decide to get back up and take responsibility for my life. I refused to let my circumstances set the thermostat for my life and finances—so I got busy.

A young woman went to her mother and told her about her life and how things were so hard for her. She did not know how she was going to make it and wanted to give up. She was tired of fighting and struggling. It seemed that as one problem was solved, a new one arose. Her mother took her to the kitchen. She filled three pots with water and placed each on a high fire. Soon the pots came to a boil. In the first, she placed carrots; in the second, she placed eggs; and in the last, she placed ground coffee beans.

She let them sit and boil, without saying a word. In about twenty minutes, she turned off the burners. She fished the carrots out and placed them in a bowl. She pulled the eggs out and placed them in a bowl. Then she ladled the coffee out and placed it in a bowl. Turning to her daughter, she asked, "Tell me, what do you see?"

"Carrots, eggs, and coffee," the young woman replied. The mother brought her closer and asked her to feel the carrots. She did and noted that they were soft. She then asked her to take an egg and break it. After pulling off the shell, the daughter observed the hard-boiled egg. Finally, she asked her to sip the coffee. The daughter smiled as she tasted its rich flavor. The daughter then asked, "What does it mean, mother?"

Her mother explained that each of these objects had faced the same adversity—boiling water—but each reacted differently. The carrot went in strong, hard, and unrelenting. However, after being subjected to the boiling water, it softened and became weak. The egg had been fragile. Its thin outer shell had protected its liquid interior. But, after sitting in the boiling water, its insides became hardened. The ground coffee beans, however, were unique. Instead of the water changing them, they had changed the water.

"Which are you?" the mother asked her daughter. "When adversity knocks on your door, how do you respond? Are you a carrot, an egg, or a coffee bean?"

Think of this: Which am I? Am I the carrot that seems strong, but with pain and adversity wilts, becomes soft, and loses its strength? Am I the egg that starts with a malleable heart, but changes with the heat? After a death, a breakup, or a financial hardship, does my shell look the same, but on the inside am I bitter and tough with a stiff spirit and a hardened heart? Or am I like the coffee bean? The bean actually changes the hot water, the very circumstance that brings the pain. When the water gets hot, it releases its fragrance and flavor.

What do you believe life is really about and holds for you? Your thoughts about life and what it holds for you are absolutely important for you to know; otherwise, very little will ever go right for you. Sometimes, people have the craziest notions about life, which keep them searching for all the wrong things in all the wrong places. Did you ever stop to think you could be in the right place searching for the wrong things?

Life is not about giving first. Uh oh! Did I say something sacrilegious? I know this perhaps goes against the grain of most people's upbringings. Now, obviously, a person can give love, but what about all the other things in life that help sustain it? Love can't pay the bills, love can't make someone successful in business, and love cannot answer every question. Love is a natural state of living, but it is not enough to provide the items necessary for life to be lived fluently.

There are many things absolutely essential for life, such as oxygen (clean air) and love; but what about food, clothing, and shelter? In the world's richest nation, there are tens of millions living in poverty without adequate shelter or proper clothing for the right season, sufficient nutrition, and the list goes on. People living without these other essentials have shorter life spans than those who enjoy the privilege of having these items. Let us not leave out how important it is to have a good education to at least supply individuals with tools that can help foster creative ways to better their lifestyles and increase their incomes. Nelson Mandela said, "Education is the most powerful weapon which you can use to change the world."

Your brain is a wonderful creation. Don't ever be afraid to change what you think and to think about what you want to change. If you give in to this fear, your brain will cease to grow. Wonderful things happen when your brain is in use. Education is an essential step on the path to professional success. As job shortages continue to coerce more competition in each field of the job market, those possessing technical knowledge, as well as administrative support professionals with strong educational backgrounds, are the ones scoring high-paying jobs. Not only does a better education aid in making more money, education also contributes to becoming more solution-oriented because it keeps your brain engaged and active.

Doing the things you would really love to do in life comes with a premium. Life is too short to waste and too long not to enjoy. They say you only live once, but I don't necessarily agree with this statement. I believe you have more chances to live than you do to die. You live daily, but you die once. While you are alive on this earth, your opportunities are limitless to do all the things you want to improve your life and to help improve the lives of others. However, once you're dead, that's it! Every chance you've ever had and did not take advantage of to make a difference ends with you making no difference at all.

So, again, I ask the question, what is life all about? First and foremost, life is about getting, followed by giving. Life is about you gathering everything you possibly can while on your journey, so what you get in life, you are able to give to others. There is no better way to expound in a simple phrase what the Bible says about this sequence. God made a promise to Abraham so he could make a difference in the lives of nations: "I will make you into a great nation and I will bless you; I will make your name great, and you will be a blessing" (Genesis 12:2). You can't give something you don't have!

How can you help the world when you have little or nothing to help the world with? Your life is a message board to those nearest to you and to the world. Part of your job is to make sure the messages of your life are inspiring to others.

Create the things you want to exist, but ignore distractions such as fear and doubt. The goal is not to live forever in this life; the goal is to create something that will last longer than you do. The secret to getting ahead is getting started. Consider these five things for you to do to get the things you want in life, so you can give the things you really want to give.

1. GO FOR THE GOLD

Why do most people feel they have to apologize for making a lot of money? One of the reasons is because they live among those who do not value money as they do. You will never influence others by trying to be like them. Don't feel bad for being glad about something you left behind.

Some family members and friends may not fully understand your drive to live your dream; but on the flip side, it's not for them to comprehend—it is for you to realize the why. How can anyone have the audacity to judge a person's desire to have a better life? Aren't these same people going to their jobs, working days on end, to get money for their families?

Get the gold by starting your business, writing your book, becoming a consultant in your field, or selling your cookies baked in your kitchen. When was the last time you lost the apprehension to do something you didn't think you could do? Believe this; you will succeed if you are crazy enough to believe you can.

2. Invest Some of Your Money

Money needs activity in order to grow. Another name for money is *currency*—it moves from one hand to the next hand, from one company to another company, and from one nation to another. Money grows as it moves, but its value is depleted when it is stationary.

You are most likely unable to invest like Warren Buffet, but you can start investing like he started—with what he had at the time. To start investing with twenty-five dollars to one hundred dollars a month is not something to feel embarrassed about. The Bible gives the best advice about starting small in Zechariah 4:10: "Do not despise this small beginning . . ." Investing is taking a small portion of what income you earn and throwing it into your future so when you arrive there, there will be more money waiting for you. Do what you know you should do now, because saying later is another way of saying never.

3. Educate Yourself

A formal college education is not the only education there is. The word "educate" simply means to impart knowledge or information by direct instruction. In fact, self-education doesn't have to mean making one mistake after another. You can purchase books, audio CDs, or videos that can educate you on how to start a business, to invest money, or even to be better at befriending others. The supply of informational transmissions is endless.

4. Aim High

Make sure your presence is missed, but even more important is to make sure that your absence is felt. If you have a job, there

Get What Life Is Holding for You

are higher positions available with higher pay grades. If being an entrepreneur is not your goal, helping one can be just as lucrative. Become an intrapreneur, which is someone who works within a business to develop an idea into a workable product. Intrapreneurs are given a high level of autonomy and flexibility for their projects by the companies they work for. An intrapreneur is often considered the person who acts fundamentally similar to an entrepreneur, but without the risks attached with being an entrepreneur.

5. Avoid Gossipers and Naysayers

If you refuse to hear the latest gossip, you are uninformed. If you hear the latest gossip, you are misinformed. The desires you have in life and the things you pursue are your own personal rights. Sharing your personal ideas for business or life can become a target for someone who doesn't want to see you succeed or wants to use your idea as their own. Some of your best and extraordinary moments in life are the ones you have to keep to yourself because they are too incredible for others to believe.

A young Jewish boy in the Bible named Joseph had a dream. This dream consumed him to the point that he shared it with his brothers and even his mother and father, who misunderstood what the dream was referring to, thinking it referred to them in a negative way. Every time you share things that may move you ahead of the line, you run the risk of being misunderstood. You are responsible for what you say, but you are not responsible for what people think you say.

I love the DIRECTV commercial, "Don't Have Your Dad Get Punched over a Can of Soup," because it depicts a sequence of possible events that can happen when the wrong choices are made. This is the transcript of this commercial:

Turn on Your Life

When the cable company keeps you on hold you feel trapped;
When you feel trapped, you need to feel free;
When you need to feel free, you try hang gliding;
When you try hang gliding, you crash into things;
When you crash into things, the grid goes down;
When the grid goes down, crime goes up;
And when crime goes up, your dad gets punched for a can of soup.
Don't have your dad get punched over a can of soup—
Get rid of cable and upgrade to DIRECTV.

This scenario may sound comical for a television commercial, but it makes the message clear. It almost describes Joseph's story, but the ending in his case was that God simply turned for good the evil his brothers intended for him.

Don't become blind to opportunities because things aren't working out the way you initially thought. Just keep your eyes open and you will see a plethora of opportunities swimming in an ocean of misfortune.

CHAPTER TWENTY

GREATNESS IS A DECISION AWAY

"Never underestimate the power of dreams and the influence
of the human spirit. We are all the same in this notion:
The potential for greatness lives within each of us."
—WILMA RUDOLPH

*A commanding officer who instructs his troops to march
into battle will never bear the weight of greatness as
does the one who leads his troops into battle.*

GREATNESS IS NOT ACHIEVED because one person was born of parents that are rich, or because your net worth rates you the richest person in the world, or due to you simply playing sports; greatness is attained because people view you as great in their sight. Individuals do not make themselves great, other people do. Greatness should never be measured by the things a person possesses, but by the quality of things a person does for others.

Horror gripped the heart of the World War I soldier as he saw his lifelong friend fall in battle. Caught in a trench with continuous gunfire whizzing over his head, the soldier asked his lieutenant if he might go out into the "no man's land" between the trenches to bring his fallen comrade back.

"You can go," said the lieutenant, "but I don't think it will be worth it. Your friend is probably dead and you may throw your life away." The lieutenant's advice didn't matter, and the soldier went anyway. Miraculously he managed to reach his friend, hoist him onto his shoulder and bring him back to their company's trench despite being shot himself. As the two of them tumbled in together to the bottom of the trench, the officer checked the wounded soldier, and then looked kindly at his friend.

"I told you it wouldn't be worth it," he said. "Your friend is dead and you are mortally wounded."

"It was worth it, though, sir," said the soldier.

"What do you mean, worth it?" responded the lieutenant. "Your friend is dead."

"Yes, sir," the private answered. "But it was worth it because when I got to him, he was still alive and I had the satisfaction of hearing him say, 'Jim, I knew you'd come.'"

In all my years of being on this planet, there is one strike of light that seems to be turned on more than in any other subject matter. And, while most people my age are thinking about retiring, I am digging deeper to fully discover myself and my true potential. The longer I live, visit other countries, and meet new people, the more I notice what appears to be a common thread among mostly everyone. This is especially true among those living in Western culture. That thread is a deep inner fear of unveiling who they really are and the things they are potentially capable of performing.

Greatness Is a Decision Away

It seems as if people are frightened of the sheer fact of being who they would really like to be. Many of these people continue to live out their years under the guise of other people's thoughts and expectations of them. This mindset is like a double-edged sword. These people are too afraid to move into the consciousness of who they truly are, and they are too terrified of losing their friends and loved ones if they move toward changing their lives. Now this is living between a rock and a hard place.

Each person must at some point in life come to the realization that they are capable of greatness. Otherwise, the greatness they are capable of will never be realized during their lifetime. This is not arrogance; there is humility in owning who you are. Greatness should be an effortless accomplishment. Instead of greatness being an effortless accomplishment, it is an absurd notion that a person of assumed limited capability can even think of achieving such a thing.

When you refuse to stand up and be noticed, you are really doing not only yourself an injustice, but the entire world. To recognize your unique status on Earth is to realize that this power is in you; however, it's just not of you. One person doesn't have less potential greatness residing in them than any other person. Everyone has different gifts. Some people use a greater portion of their gifts, which causes them to appear extraordinary. However, they are the same gift, but with greater usage of ability.

Reflect for a moment on the people who have exploded out of the framework of unadulterated possibility by using the one thing that came natural to them and exploiting it to help humanity. Consider such names as Abraham Lincoln, Albert Einstein, Martin Luther King Jr., and Ben Franklin. Now picture your name among this list.

It is hard to imagine all the extraordinary talent that has gone unacknowledged among belittled people. Consider African

Americans and women, whose talents have been suppressed in American history because conditions have not allowed for such possibility to be showcased. Think of the talent in all people, regardless of race or color—abilities yet to be seen on this planet.

I believe that each person has arrived at this moment, for such a time as this . . . to make a difference instead of continuing to make no difference at all. Difference makers will develop mentally by first accepting their own greatness without comparison and by believing in the inherent power God has placed in them. But the first person who has to listen to you is you.

Speak out loud, make yourself known, and shine brightly. Even the Bible says to let your light shine. Shine your spotlight on someone and rescue them from the darkness of their self-defeated mentality. Arise; for the glory of God has risen upon you.

CHAPTER TWENTY-ONE

IT TAKES EVERYTHING TO WIN

"Winning is a habit. Unfortunately, so is losing."
—Vince Lombardi

You will never realize how great you can be until you become so hungry to succeed that you lose the fear to fail.

As I watched game seven of the NBA 2013 Finals between the San Antonio Spurs and the Miami Heat, I saw both teams display resilience and mental toughness throughout the course of the game. My thought was that a loss on either side would come down to one individual breaking down during the last seconds of the game. I knew the person who mentally broke down and made mistakes would not be a bad player, per se, but one who had not consistently played well throughout the series. Unfortunately, that player was Manu Ginóbili.

Whether a team wins or loses, it is still a team. However, the individual player on a team who isn't mentally hungry and composed enough to want to do anything and everything to win, will allow their opponent to push back their mental and physical limitations. Moreover, that person is just as responsible for the team's loss as is the team itself.

I heard LeBron James in an interview after winning the seventh game of the NBA 2013 Finals say, "The Spurs are a great team that pushed us to new limits." In a nutshell, what LeBron James was saying was that his internal hunger to defeat the San Antonio Spurs became more intense during the game. It made him play smarter and harder than he's ever played, dig deeper inside himself than he's ever internally dug, and fight harder than he's ever fought before. My friend, this is what champions are made of.

In my many years of studying human behavior, under the auspices of both a counselor and a religious leader, I have discovered that people, in and of themselves, do not determine how far they can go or how much they can take. Neither can they determine the extent to which they are willing to sacrifice without something or someone coercing them to either their breaking point or their refusal-to-break point. Being pushed and shoved to exceed their personal limits demonstrates how people's personal boundaries are not necessarily determined by them, as much as by their willingness to triumph against the person or challenge that is poised to conquer them.

Your internal drive and determination to win in life, sports, or business is not accelerated by the limits you have set but by the challenge that pushes you to reposition the line of your capability in order to just overcome. This is usually the story behind every great person who discovered that the boundary they set was only established because they had no opponent or challenge to impel

It Takes Everything to Win

them to reestablish their limits. The collage of negative thoughts that bombard people after a poor performance, whether in life, sports, or business, has but one aim—and that aim is to discourage and batter them until they find themselves rehearsing the mistakes that they are so desperately trying not to repeat. There can be no victories without encountering conflict. Whoever concedes to the pressures of life or the abilities of their competitor cannot exceed the limits they have personally set for themselves.

What are the limits you may have unconsciously determined for yourself? Are you having a difficult time trying to find the motivation to go to the next level of life or business? The greatest evidence of your desire to win is displayed in your greatest desire to sacrifice. The results are locked away in the effort. You cannot shirk the personal responsibility of stagnation. Avoiding opportunities that challenge your skill set will never get you moving up in the ranks of life—rather, assuming you've done enough to stay ahead will result in a loss of momentum. You have to be willing to pay less today for something that will increase in cost later. If you avoid paying less today, be sure of this one thing: it will cost you far more tomorrow.

Winning is hard against a worthy opponent . . . and it should be. Yet winning is even harder when you don't want to fight in the first place. Striving for perfection is self-defeating, but striving to become better at what you do is one step up the ladder of development. What you must do to ultimately achieve your triumph or victory is to understand the power of patience and perseverance. You cannot look at the end of the road as though it is right around the corner. Your mind has to be set for a marathon, not a sprint.

Make no mistake; everything worth fighting for is worth the price of admission. From being married to having children to living your dream, anything of value is worth all the fight and tenacity you can muster in order to come out on the other side. If you think that you can simply live your life without suffering harm, casualties, or defeat, you are sadly mistaken. You cannot sit back and expect the world to bow at your feet without you having to conquer its challenges.

Michael Jordan won six NBA Championships with the Chicago Bulls but was often undermined by Jerry Krause, the team's general manager, in his own attempts to keep Michael humble. In one unofficial meeting, Jerry Krause said, "Michael, there is no 'I' in team." Michael Jordan's reply was, "Yeah, but there is an 'I' in win."

Whether the problems you face are as part of a team, as an individual, or both, the "I" (you) is the only one required to demand the deep passion and hunger to win in life. You cannot demand it from anyone else; you must demand it from yourself!

If you truly want something out of life, do not ask someone whether you can have it. Their choice will always be to give you less of what they have because, to them, that is all you deserve. The only thing that stands between you and what you want from life is the faith to believe it is possible and that you deserve it.

CHAPTER TWENTY-TWO
Live Life NOW!

> "To live is to choose. But to choose well, you must know who you are and what you stand for, where you want to go and why you want to get there."
> —Kofi Annan

If you had the power to choose either to be rich or to live your life's dream, which would you choose?

ONE OF THE GREATEST MEN I have ever had the privilege of knowing was Dr. Turnel Nelson. He was not only a mentor to me, but also my spiritual father. He taught me many things in our years together, and his greatest lesson for me was in how he illustrated living in the face of a sentence to die. As he became ill with cancer, he never accepted a cease-and-desist order for living. In fact, he would often say, "Don't die full; die empty! Reach for all you can reach for, accomplish all you can accomplish, touch as many people as possible, and know God by living for Him." Dr. Nelson traveled extensively, with over a hundred and fifty speaking

Turn on Your Life

engagements a year. And, every place he went, he emptied himself of what was in him to give to his audience.

When he died, world leaders, both secular and Christian, attended his homegoing. It was said by his eulogizer, a longtime friend of Dr. Nelson's, that "Turnel simply ran so fast through life that he emptied himself before he knew it." He traveled and ministered the gospel all around the globe, and no one was more loved.

This is not a time to survive, but to strive. It is not the time to sit down, but to stand up. This is not a time to be silent, but to speak up and speak out. Command your life; it is to serve you, not for you to serve it. You have a choice to make—and that is to live or die. You must decide to live life on purpose, no matter what the cost. Every breath you take should be a choice to live. Every time you inhale, you should breathe in the life you so desperately desire; and every time you exhale, it should be the energy you employ to be completely engaged in making sure your life is worth living. Leonardo da Vinci said, "While I thought that I was learning how to live, I have been learning how to die."

You were not designed to live a life of total stress and vain accomplishments. Life is supposed to matter; it is supposed to be celebrated, not just tolerated. Although there are things in life that may cause you to lose a sense of focus, never let life itself get out of focus. Life matters, and to live life should be a matter of NOW, not later.

I personally mentor over one hundred business owners, professional athletes and coaches, and personnel in upper management positions. Several of my client-friends are in the NBA coaching ranks, and when I visit their cities, I often attend their games, mixing business with pleasure. One day, I asked my seven-year-old son, who so happens to be a basketball junkie, if he was interested in attending a Chicago Bulls game and visiting the locker room afterward or if he would like to fly to Los Angeles to attend a Lakers game. He looked at me with the most serious seven-year-old stare, as if he was thinking, "How dare you make me choose." When he opened his mouth to respond, he said one word: "Both!" Then he went back to eating his cereal.

My wife and I looked at each other as if to say, "The audacity of this kid!" Yet my son realized that he wasn't limited to a choice between this and that, or to choosing one over the other. It was, for him, bigger than that. He understood that he possessed the power to choose both. So I called one of the Chicago Bulls coaches, who I mentor, and informed him that I was coming to Chicago for both business and pleasure and I was bringing my wife and youngest son. He provided tickets for all three of us and my son absolutely enjoyed the game. Unfortunately, football season was over for the Dallas Cowboys, but next season, he'll get to attend one of the Dallas Cowboys games as well. Who said you can't have your cake and eat it, too? I guess it doesn't apply to my son, or does it?

Do not allow life to just throw things at you as if you ought to feel lucky that anything came your way at all. Yes, life has some unfortunate circumstances, but there are fortunes concealed in every one of them. You should not spend your life avoiding every situation, because difficult situations allow you to grow. Every human being living on this planet has an almost gravitational pull to these situations in order to go through them, not just to go to them.

Albert Camus once said, "I would rather live my life as if there is a God and die to find out there isn't, than live my life as if there isn't and die to find out there is." Death is one of the most certain things in life, and most people are not ready for it. However, life

Turn on Your Life

is more certain than death, and people don't seem to be ready for it, either. You have to be alive in order to die.

Are you living to empty yourself—determined to fulfill your life's mission? Or are you on a slow pace with no direction, hoping to stumble onto the end because you feel that your life has no purpose? Snap out of it! Gird yourself up and get ready for life. You have places to see, people to meet, businesses to start, and expectations to fulfill. We've been given a brand-new life and have everything to live for, including a future—and that future starts NOW!

CHAPTER TWENTY-THREE

Making Good Business Cents

"Something in human nature causes us to start slacking off at our moment of greatest accomplishment. As you become successful, you will need a great deal of self-discipline not to lose your sense of balance, humility, and commitment."
—H. Ross Perot

If you have any business sense, it better make cents or it makes no sense at all.

THREE YOUNG MEN were once given three kernels of corn apiece by a wise old sage, who admonished them to go out into the world and use the corn to bring themselves good fortune. The first young man put his three kernels of corn into a bowl of hot broth and ate them.

The second thought, "I can do better than that," and he planted his three kernels of corn. Within a few months, he had three stalks of corn. He took the ears of corn from the stalks, boiled them, and had enough corn for several meals.

The third man said to himself, "I can do better than that!" He also planted his three kernels of corn, but when his three stalks of corn produced, he stripped one of the stalks and replanted all of the seeds in it, gave the second stalk of corn to a sweet maiden, and ate the third.

His one full stalk's worth of replanted corn kernels gave him two hundred stalks of corn! And the kernels of these he continued to replant, setting aside only a bare minimum to eat. He eventually planted a hundred acres of corn. With his fortune, he not only won the hand of the sweet maiden but purchased the land owned by the sweet maiden's father.

And he never hungered again.

I have had the wonderful honor of speaking to many business owners about the durability of their companies during today's critical financial times. And 87 percent of them believe that despite government attempts to pull the American economy out of the dumps, they can read the handwriting on the wall, and it's not good. It is absolutely vital for owners of companies to make as much sense as possible as to what will and will not work during these dreadful economic conditions or else their companies will make no cents at all.

Families all over this globe are struggling to make ends meet. New research indicates that nearly a quarter of a million people in Ireland have nothing left to live on after they have paid their bills each month. The latest national snapshot of the social segment shows the number of Australians being turned away from emergency relief, disability, homeless, and youth welfare services is dramatically on the rise. Figures from the Australian Council of Social Service show that demand for emergency relief, including food and shelter, almost doubled in 2008 to 2009 from the previous financial year (Erin Long, *Sunshine Daily Coast*, April 20, 2011).

> "MORE people are struggling to make ends meet and the demand for support services is growing as the cost of living grows.
>
> The latest national snapshot of the social sector shows the number of Australians being turned away from emergency relief, disability, homeless and youth welfare services is dramatically on the rise.
>
> Figures from the Australian Council of Social Service show that demand for emergency relief, including food and shelter, almost doubled in 2009-10 from the previous financial year.
>
> Even more worryingly, the number of people being turned away without getting help is increasing.
>
> ACOSS CEO Cassandra Goldie said the figures were concerning.
>
> We are seeing an enormous strain on community welfare groups who are struggling to meet the growing demand, she said.
>
> It's a worrying picture, challenging our notion of a fair and egalitarian society.
>
> On the Sunshine Coast, service providers in Nambour who support low-income earners, the unemployed or homeless are experiencing the biggest demand for their services in years.
>
> The Lions Emergency Accommodation Centre in Carroll St is one of the service providers struggling to keep up with demand. . . ."

Minimum wage is rising, trying to stay up with inflation, and small businesses are finding that there is just not enough money to go around. While businesses are trying to remain or become solvent, banks are not helping struggling businesses by not lending or tightening restrictions for businesses to borrow. Banks, like all other businesses, are required to make profits. In order to answer to their regulators and their shareholders, banks must be profitable or they cease to exist. That's exactly what is happening today with small businesses as well.

The American public was informed by the US Government when trying to pass the Stimulus Package through Congress to bail out the US economy and housing market that the bulk of the stimulus money would not be spent until the end of 2010, at which point it would probably not be needed, and funds can be redirected back into the hands of the tax payers. This, of course, was not the case, and unemployment is still increasing at an alarming rate. Today, the US population has very little confidence in its government. Politicians give their speeches of no more taxes, but they continue to break these promises because they just can't figure out any other way of truly rectifying our economy. In order to increase employment, they must stimulate small businesses and encourage banks to lend. Yet the US government today does not seem to have this as a priority.

Business owners and heads of families must pay close attention to markets and strongly consider how they manage and spend their money. Businesses should be especially sensitive to consumers' new spending trends and be on the cutting edge of how to sell more products without increasing their prices. Customers will become loyal when they think that businesses are considerate of their needs as well.

More people are starting home-based businesses, and even children are cashing in on their ideas. Take Richie Stachowski, for example. When he was only eleven, he and his family went to Hawaii on vacation, and while Richie was out snorkeling with his father and was so thrilled by the numbers and colors of the fish he kept seeing that he wanted to be able to shout to his dad each time he saw something new, but there was no way for him to do that. So, Richie set about becoming an inventor. After a month of modifications, his underwater megaphone invention was a complete success, allowing people to talk to each other underwater from up to fifteen feet away.

There are so many ways you can make more money and be free from the prison of debt. Is money the primary pursuit? Of course not. However, it is the single tool to help improve your quality of life. Creativeness is the key to starting a business, and networking is a way to keep it moving. Think of the various things you can do to make more money and do not be afraid to challenge yourself in whatever you decide to attempt.

Five Things that Constitute Good Business Sense

1. **Exhibit Character**
   Character is something you either have or are. People of preference try to make something *for* themselves, while a person of character works to make something *of* themselves and their businesses.
2. **Forget the Past**
   The past is always going to be the way it was. Stop trying to change the past. Stop looking at where you have been and

start looking at where you can be. Plan for future profits instead of going over past losses.

3. **Don't Procrastinate**
   A procrastinator is always paying more for something they could have paid less for if they would have made a decision yesterday. Ask yourself, "If I don't take action now, what will it cost me tomorrow?"

4. **Know Your Business**
   Too many people know what they are running from, but not many know what they are running to. Concentrate on finding your business purpose, then concentrate on fulfilling it.

5. **Know Your Customers**
   When you have what people need, you have customers. Needs are not hard to discover. Find what your customers are looking for by asking the ton of questions you need to ask. If you want to get help to increase your profit margin, ask questions to potential customers. You will be surprised how they will provide you with answers on how to make them buy from you. Make your customer your friend, because people rarely buy from people they don't like.

I know how money can be tight, but I am also aware of how tight some people can be with money. Don't allow the lack of money to cause you to be a tightwad. See your money as a seed, and plant it into your ideas.

CHAPTER TWENTY-FOUR
Missing "U"

"My dad was my best friend and greatest role model. He was an amazing dad, coach, mentor, soldier, husband, and friend."
—Tiger Woods

How important you are is not contingent on the significance others may have placed on your life. The fact that you are here on this earth suggests that you are important to the world.

A YOUNG MAN learns what's most important in life from the guy next door. It had been some time since Jack had seen the old man. College, girls, career, and life itself got in the way. In fact, Jack moved clear across the country in pursuit of his dreams. There, in the rush of his busy life, Jack had little time to think about the past and often no time to spend with his wife and son. He was working on his future and nothing could stop him.

Over the phone his mother told him, "Mr. Belser died last night. The funeral is Wednesday."

Turn on Your Life

Memories flashed through his mind like an old newsreel as he sat quietly remembering his childhood days.

"Jack, did you hear me?"

"Oh sorry, Mom. Yes, I heard you. It's been so long since I thought of him. I'm sorry, but I honestly thought he died years ago," Jack said.

"Well, he didn't forget you. Every time I saw him he'd ask how you were doing. He'd reminisce about the many days you spent over 'his side of the fence,' as he put it," Mom told him.

"I loved that old house he lived in," Jack said.

"You know, Jack, after your father died, Mr. Belser stepped in to make sure you had a man's influence in your life," she said.

"He's the one who taught me carpentry," he said. "I wouldn't be in this business if it wasn't for him. He spent a lot of time teaching me things he thought were important. Mom, I'll be there for the funeral," Jack said.

As busy as he was, he kept his word. Jack caught the next flight to his hometown. Mr. Belser's funeral was small and uneventful. He had no children of his own, and most of his relatives had passed away.

The night before he had to return home Jack and his mom stopped by to see the old house next door one more time.

Standing in the doorway Jack paused for a moment. It was like crossing over into another dimension, a leap through space and time. The house was exactly as he remembered. Every step held memories. Every picture, every piece of furniture . . . Jack stopped suddenly.

"What's wrong, Jack?" his mom asked.

"The box is gone," he said.

"What box?" Mom asked.

"There was a small gold box that he kept locked on top of his desk. I must have asked him a thousand times what was inside. All he'd ever tell me was, 'The thing I value most,'" Jack said.

It was gone. Everything about the house was exactly how Jack remembered it except for the box. He figured someone from the Belser family had taken it.

"Now I'll never know what was so valuable to him," Jack said, "I better get some sleep. I have an early flight home, Mom."

It had been about two weeks since Mr. Belser died. Returning home from work one day, Jack discovered a note in his mailbox. "Signature required on a package. No one at home. Please stop by the main post office within the next three days," the note read.

Early the next day Jack retrieved the package. The package was old and looked like it had been mailed a hundred years ago. The handwriting was difficult to read, but the return address caught his attention.

"Mr. Harold Belser," it read.

Jack took the package out to his car and ripped it open. There inside was the gold box and an envelope. Jack's hands shook as he read the note inside.

"Upon my death please forward this box and its contents to Jack Bennett. It's the thing I value most in my life." A small key was taped to the letter. His heart raced as tears filled his eyes. Jack carefully unlocked the box. There inside he found a beautiful gold pocket watch.

Running his fingers slowly over the finely etched casing, he unlatched the cover. Inside he found these words engraved:

"Jack, Thanks for your time! —Harold Belser."

"The thing he valued most . . . was . . . my time."

Jack held the watch for a few minutes, then called his office and cleared his appointments for the next two days. "Why?" Janet, his assistant, asked. "I need some time to spend with my son," he said. "Oh, by the way, Janet, thanks for your time".

—Story by Bob Perks

It has been said that if the letter U were removed from the alphabet, the English language would lose over three thousand words. In defining what I believe is a critical element of creative, effective writing, I think about the famous quote from *Animal Farm*: "All words are equal, but some words are more equal than others." Among the top ten most powerful words in the English language is one word that stands supreme.

Before I say what this word is, let me suggest to you that if the letter U were to disappear from the English language, it would point to the reality of how crucial some things are.

The word that I believe is unequivocally more powerful and equal than others is "you." Most people would rather say "you" over "I" because "you" takes all the responsibility and/or focus off of themselves. The amazing power behind "you" is that it can refer to anyone. In a speech or in writing, the word is so cleverly used that it causes a person to take stock of what is being shared. Think of statements such as "You are powerful!"; "You can do it!"; "You are amazing!"; "You can be great!"; "You can be rich!"; and "You are my hero!" Can these words help facilitate a more powerful sense of self? Absolutely.

Some people say that others are dispensable and can easily be replaced. I strongly disagree with this statement because I believe that a person is indispensable and can never be replaced. "People" refers to the plural, but a "person" conveys the singular. You are so important to the natural balance of this universe that if you were not here millions of incidents would be missing from history. Think for one moment of how many people you have touched during your lifetime, how many lives you have inadvertently inspired, or the differences you have made in the lives of children. Some people wouldn't be married had you not introduced them to each other. You may never know in this lifetime how people were touched by your life or words or how many business ideas or inventions you may have inspired. It would be staggering to know how many things would be different today if you were missing from the mind of God.

You are important, you are necessary, you are great, and if you feel that you are not, just think retrospectively of the people in your life. The movie *It's A Wonderful Life* with James Stewart is one of my favorite movies because it shows how important one single life can be on this earth. Whenever you are tempted to think that you are insignificant, remember how many words would be missing if the letter U were removed from the alphabet.

CHAPTER TWENTY-FIVE
NEED A BOOST OR A BOOT?

"No student ever attains very eminent success by simply doing what is required of him: it is the amount and excellence of what is over and above the required that determines the greatness of ultimate distinction."
—CHARLES KENDALL ADAMS

If someone gives you a boot (a swift kick in the butt) instead of a boost to get started, what does it matter as long as you are on your way somewhere?

I ONCE LISTENED TO A SPEECH by John Madden as he spoke briefly about attending a coaches' camp held by Vince Lombardi. First of all, he thought that he was not going to get much out of the camp because he had already reached the top of his game by becoming the head coach of a professional NFL team. He felt that his credentials were extensive enough to get him the position and that there wasn't much Coach Lombardi could teach him. He sat through the morning session as Vince Lombardi taught on one play for the entire morning. He thought that surely Vince was going to expand and go into other plays that could help him in coaching. When all the coaches returned for the afternoon session, Vince Lombardi continued his teaching on the same single play. Coach Lombardi explained that one football play so extensively, and from every angle, that John Madden became mesmerized. He said that after hearing Coach Lombardi teach on one play for the entire day, he realized that he didn't know as much about football as he thought he did.

Oftentimes, pride and ignorance can masquerade as self-confidence, and it can rob you of your growth. You may think that you know all there is to know about your particular field because you are now riding among the ranks with others who have been in your field far longer than you have; but getting there is entirely different from staying there.

A swift kick in the butt by someone who pays no attention to your accolades may be all that is needed to get you going. You have to remember that it's not how good you are, it's how good you want to be. Yet greatness cannot be achieved by simply following in the steps of great men and women. If you follow in someone else's steps, your personal success will only reflect the accomplishments of the one whose footprints you choose to follow. You will simply become a carbon copy of a great original. And while following a person with impressive qualities that you desire to emulate does not guarantee greatness, it can help you recognize it. Eventually, you will have to veer off and blaze your own trail.

I have learned a great deal during my years under the tutelage of great men, and one valuable lesson is that you cannot simply trace the steps of great mentors, following them to their ends, because at the conclusion of their course, you will only discover your mentor's destiny—not your own.

Imagine a rocket ship going into orbit; attached to it is a booster engine. The booster is designed to help the rocket get into space until it can fire up its own engine, detach from the booster, and continue its mission and fulfill its purpose. You are the rocket ship, and your mentor is the booster engine—only meant to get you to where you can take off on your own.

The power exemplified in the booster engine is the many years of experience and the enormous amount of knowledge and wisdom you can acquire from your mentor. Great leaders and mentors want nothing more than to pass on their wealth of knowledge and to help propel others to achieve more in their lifetimes than the mentors may have accomplished in theirs.

Understanding this can be the difference between you wasting your energy or preserving it. The booster engine is attached so that the rocket ship can conserve as much energy as possible because its mission will be quite arduous. The rocket ship uses quite a bit of fuel just getting off the ground. However, the rocket ship needs to also preserve its fuel so that it can be used in space and during its return to Earth—and this is where the booster engine comes in.

A father, mother, mentor, or pastor can be your booster engine whose sole purpose is to help you excel. It is presumed that you respect the presence and recognize the magnitude and enormity of the mentor's wisdom and knowledge. If not, you will never fully adhere to the instructions that can help you build your personal life or business.

Wise and successful people are in such demand that a protégé should always consider their time as highly valuable. Most people are young in knowledge and experience (which does not mean that these people are necessarily young in age), and it can be easy to think that successful people have nothing else to do but to listen to a bumbling idiot voice his or her knowledge about nothing.

My solemn recommendation for people seeking wise counsel from someone who is successful is to ask your question, shut up, and remember to pay attention while you are in the presence of greatness. Words from the lips of a wise man or woman are like pillars that can support your next level in life or business. They will help you discover your worth and maintain your value.

To desire greatness is a lofty thought, not a bad one. Usually, people who have achieved greatness did not ask for it, nor did they actually realize that they had obtained it. Great leaders are great givers, and unless you are willing to tax your time, energy, and resources, you simply will want the title of greatness at other people's expense.

Dr. Martin Luther King Jr., Nelson Mandela, and Vince Lombardi are men I would love to talk to, if they were alive today. One was a preacher and civil rights leader; another was a freedom fighter, prisoner, and first black president of a democratic South Africa; and the other was arguably the greatest football coach in the National Football League. The vastness of their knowledge concerning winning was extraordinary. Developing strategies to win at anything and executing that strategy is pertinent to winning in life. These three men were from different ends of the spectrum but so very much alike. All three of them believed in the power of people working as one, they believed in using drastic measures to achieve their goals, and they all gave their lives to what they believed. These three extraordinary men never separated what they did in life from their life. You are what you do, and what you do speaks volumes as to who you are.

Average success is often based on setting average goals. Decide what you really want: to be the best, the fastest, the strongest, the biggest . . . whatever. Aim for the ultimate. Decide where you want to end up. Make that your goal. Then you can work backward and lay out every step along the way. Never start small where goals are concerned. You'll make better decisions—and find it much easier to work a lot harder—when your ultimate goal is ultimate success. Nevertheless, you must embrace the voice of a mentor who can help you achieve your personal best. I can tell you this: you will not start off at the top. Don't expect to.

Wayne Dyer said, "Successful people make money. It's not that people who make money become successful, but that successful people attract money. They bring success to what they do." People of average ability sometimes achieve outstanding success because they experience the benefit of having someone who is able to help them uncover their hidden potential. Incredibly, these people achieve more and succeed simply because they are determined to.

CHAPTER TWENTY-SIX

LIFE'S PURPOSE IS DISCOVERED WHILE HELPING OTHERS FIND THEIRS

"He has a right to criticize, who has a heart to help."
—ABRAHAM LINCOLN

Your greatest deterrent to experiencing success in any area of your life is your inability to remain focused on the chief cause that allows you to walk in success. If you can easily be pulled away from helping others, then you have already lost in the process.

LIFE WILL NEVER BE ENJOYABLE if a person cannot see the benefit in helping others succeed in accomplishing their goals; while at the same time allowing others help them succeed at achieving their own goals.

Once, a group of fifty people was attending a seminar.

Suddenly the speaker stopped and started giving each person a balloon. Each one was asked to write his or her name on it using

Turn on Your Life

a marker pen. Then all the balloons were collected and put in another room.

Now these delegates were let in that room and asked to find the balloon which had their name written on it, within five minutes.

Everyone was frantically searching for their name, pushing, colliding with each other, and there was utter chaos.

At the end of five minutes, no one could find their own balloon.

Now each one was asked to randomly collect a balloon and give it to the person whose name was written on it. Within minutes everyone had their own balloon.

The speaker began: This is exactly what is happening in our lives. Everyone is frantically looking for happiness all around, not knowing where it is. Our happiness lies in the happiness of other people. Give them their happiness, you will get your own happiness.

And this is the purpose of human life.

What do Dr. Ben Carson, Donald Trump, Michael Jordan, Warren Buffet, Oprah Winfrey, Mark Victor Hansen, and Tiger Woods all have in common?

You may think the answer is that they are all rich and famous. And, you are absolutely correct. You could say that each of these individuals has achieved something notable. I will not argue with you about that. However, there is something else that they all have in common . . . a quality that these and other not-so-rich-and-famous people have acquired. They have all discovered the one personal characteristic that billions of people have yet to discover.

People spend their entire lives thinking of what could make them happy. Regrettably, over 90 percent of the population thinks having more than enough money would make them the happiest people on the planet. I personally differ with that opinion. I am not saying that these people do not know what they want, but that they haven't the faintest idea of what they need to actually fulfill their lives. The only reason an overwhelming percentage of the population, especially those living in the United States, feels like money is the solution to their misery is because they have not discovered their true passion. Hundreds of people have won hundreds of thousands and even tens to hundreds of millions of dollars in some lottery game, and yet in five years or less, close to 80 percent of those winners go broke.

The previous list of people I mentioned have one thing in common, and it's not money: it's that they have discovered the "one thing" that lights up their eyes more than money itself. Money is important, but not that important. It's just unfortunate that, in this nation, money is how we keep score. Purpose, destiny, passion, and a dream are more valuable than money itself to those who breathe their "one thing." It is what keeps them getting up in the morning when nothing is going right for them.

When you realize what it is you were created to do, you'll find that you would rather be happy in the right place doing what you believe is your life's calling, with hardly anything going right for you at that moment, than to be in the wrong place and feeling miserable when everything is picture perfect. You can never be yourself until you know yourself. In the words of Quincy Jones, "The people who make it to the top—whether they're musicians, or great chefs, or corporate honchos—are addicted to their calling . . . [they] are the ones who'd be doing whatever it is they love, even if they weren't being paid." Unfortunately, everyone who is aware of what they are designed by the Creator to do in his or her life isn't always in love with the idea of doing it. However, they realize that their calling is a must, not a should. What brings joy to performing your life's purpose is when you are helping others at the same time you are helping yourself.

Have you discovered what it is you were called to do? Some people have an inkling of their true calling, but for them there are too many obstacles, too many distractions, and too many people standing in their way. The cost is too much, and they have too much to lose. People who thinks like this are usually people who only want to succeed with no assistance from others; but real life doesn't work like this. Each successful person, can trace their success back to some mentor, friend, or teacher who helped steer them through challenges while on their way to success.

Dr. Martin Luther King Jr., said something so profound in one of his speeches that when I read it, it dropped deep within my soul and exploded, and I have never recovered from this truth, nor do I ever want to recover. Dr. King's words helped me to focus my life with purpose and to escape the mediocrity of a blurred vision:

> "Deep down in our nonviolent creed is the conviction there are some things so dear, some things so precious, some things so eternally true, that they're worth dying for. And if a man happens to be thirty-six-years-old, as I happen to be, some great truth stands before the door of his life—some great opportunity to stand up for that which is right.
>
> A man might be afraid his home will get bombed, or he's afraid that he will lose his job, or he's afraid that he will get shot, or beat down by state troopers, and he may go on and live until he's eighty. He's just as dead at thirty-six as he would be at eighty."

Never, ever apologize for doing what you love and what you believe you are sentenced to do, even if what you love doesn't meet the specifications of a loved one. Never settle for a paycheck to ignore your passion . . . which has no equal value to your dream-worth. And never let anyone talk you out of what you believe God has placed deep down in your heart. What you know to do in your heart has greater value and purpose than what you think others want you to do with your life.

If I were you, I would not rest from my search of discovering my purpose until I was totally convinced of what I was created to perform on this planet; otherwise, life just will not have the same worth. Sometimes, a person can find their purpose in life after helping others find theirs.

Do you truly know what you want? If not, how will you recognize it when it appears? Do not be afraid to identify every detail you envision in your mind. It is your life, and you ought to know how you want it to be. Invest whatever is necessary to create the environment you want to surround you. Always see rejection as a door, not a wall. Accept the challenge and go on the hunt for your "one thing."

CHAPTER TWENTY-SEVEN
THE PLATINUM LIFE DISCOVERY

"I am here for a purpose and that purpose is to grow into a mountain, not to shrink to a grain of sand. Henceforth will I apply ALL my efforts to become the highest mountain of all and I will strain my potential until it cries for mercy."
—OG MANDINO

Making life count for something meaningful occurs when you endeavor to make a life worth living.

A LITTLE BOY TELLS HIS GRANDMA how everything is going wrong: nothing in school, in his family, or with his friends is going the way he wants it to. Meanwhile, his grandma is baking a cake. She asks her grandson if he would like a snack, which of course he does.

"Here, have some cooking oil," she says.

"Yuck," says the boy.

"Then how about a couple of raw eggs?"

"Gross, Grandma!" he replies.

Turn on Your Life

"Would you prefer some flour then? Or maybe some baking soda?" she asks.

"Grandma, those are all yucky!" he replies.

"Yes," his grandma responds, "all those things seem to taste bad all by themselves. But when they are mixed together in the right amounts and the right manner, they make a delicious cake!

"God works the same way. Many times we wonder why he would let us go through such bad and difficult times. But God knows that when he puts these things all in his order, they always work for good! We just have to trust him and, eventually, they will all make something wonderful!"

I believe there are two primary reasons most people live their entire lives in the dark concerning their true purposes. Oftentimes, these reasons compel them to go on a futile search, because there is no chance of finding what they are looking for while they are under their old mental regime. Not only are many of these people making constant blunders with their lives, but they find themselves always moving from one job to another or from marriage to marriage because their inward compasses are out of balance. Life for these people is one big earthly laboratory experiment, and they are the guinea pigs.

One reason people are unable to discover their true purpose is that they mistaken what they like to do as their primary purpose, when in fact it is their subpurpose. The second reason is similar to the first: they are unwilling to give up searching among places, peoples, and religions, believing that these entities are the most likely places they can find their purposes, when in fact they should be looking inside of themselves.

The Platinum Life Discovery

Bruce Lee, one of the greatest martial artists who ever lived, was once asked by a master martial artist to teach him everything he knew about the martial arts. Bruce Lee held up two cups, both filled with liquid, and said, "The first cup represents all your knowledge about the martial arts, and the second cup represents all my knowledge about the martial arts. If you want to fill your cup with all of my knowledge about the martial arts, you must first empty your cup of your knowledge of the martial arts."

Self-discovery comes at the price of first surrendering all the knowledge you once deemed necessary, even though these experiences made you who you are today. If you want to learn about what your true primary purpose is in life, you must empty yourself of all the false purposes you've been taught. This includes the idea that you have no purpose at all.

While you are in search of the "why" of your being, life is in constant transition. I know how it feels to harbor thoughts of wanting to do one hundred different things to define your purpose—you just can't seem to settle on the one thing you want to do more than anything in the world. Sometimes, this mental block exists because self-knowledge can be painful, and you prefer the gratification of an illusion. If most people remain ignorant of themselves, it is because they want to.

The low road to take is to simply ignore any intuition that life holds for you more than just you occupying an employment status. This is not to insinuate that one having a nine-to-five job is one having a low self-esteem. My aim is not to reduce a job to something undesirable by normal standards. Life can be just as fulfilling working for others as a person owning a business in order to provide for their family. However, if your true desire is to own your own company to provide a service to the public, why not do it? The high peak of knowledge is perfect self-knowledge, that you believe you are not a mistake and that you are wonderfully and uniquely created by your Creator for His purpose. God never creates mistakes. There is no self-definition without God-recognition. It may display wisdom to know others, but it is enlightenment to know yourself.

I want you to do something, an exercise that could help you discover your purpose in life. It is important that you understand that despite the games played with others, you must not play games with yourself. Get a blank sheet of white paper and write as the header, "My Life's Purpose." Underneath the header, start to write a list of things that matter most to you about what you believe your purpose is. Don't overthink it—just start listing things. Once you have completed your list, go through and read the items. Anything that elicits feelings of contentment, feelings of mediocrity, is not really your purpose in life—it is a substitute. Anything that elicits strong emotions, that fills you with passion, however, is certain to be where your purpose lies.

David Green, owner of Hobby Lobby, is on Forbes' list of billionaires. Growing up poor, Green learned to get the most out of everything. The company he founded still helps people do that. In 1970, Green took a $600 loan and started a business in his garage called Greco Products, assembling and selling miniature picture frames, capitalizing on a decorating fad of the time. By August 1972, the business had thrived to such an extent that Green was able to open his first store, which had three hundred square feet of retail space. Now, Green has more than 430 stores in thirty-five states, and all because he strongly believes in purpose. The son of a minister coming from generations of ministers, Green decided to do his preaching and touching lives in a different way; his goal now is to get Bibles into the hands of as many people as possible. When he discovered his purpose, he found his provision that helped him fulfill his purpose on a daily basis.

The Platinum Life Discovery

Imagine your life as a novel and your purpose as a novelty. Let me explain what I mean by this. A novel is a fictional prose work with a relatively long and often complex plot, usually divided into chapters or episodes, in which the story traditionally develops through the thoughts and actions of its character(s). Now, understand that your life deals with chapters that include daily real-life episodes. Each day, you have the opportunity to take your life in the direction you want it to go. However, a novelty is something new, original, and different that is interesting or exciting, though often for only a short time. Life holds purpose; it is supposed to work fluently, despite the bumps and turns, highs and lows—these are parts of life's obstacle course. When your purpose is discovered, its treasure is worth more than life itself.

You may not reach billionaire status or even millionaire status, but your status will count for something. Look to help others, use your creative genius to make life better for someone else, and you will see that the same people you look to benefit will reward you in turn.

Most people who are billionaires have come to a place where money makes life easy for themselves and their families, but there must be a greater cause for it. To make money is not a sin, but to do nothing with it for the sake of humanity is the greatest sin of all.

CHAPTER TWENTY-EIGHT

THE FAILURES OF THE SUCCESSFUL

"The poor, the unsuccessful, the unhappy, the unhealthy are the ones who use the word tomorrow the most."
—ROBERT KIYOSAKI

People seem to know how not to succeed without any guidance from the "How Not to Succeed" experts.

ONCE THERE WAS A KING who received a gift of two magnificent falcons. They were peregrine falcons, the most beautiful birds he had ever seen. He gave the precious birds to his head falconer to be trained.

Months passed, and one day the head falconer informed the king that though one of the falcons was flying majestically, soaring high in the sky, the other bird had not moved from its branch since the day it had arrived.

The king summoned healers and sorcerers from all the land to tend to the falcon, but no one could make the bird fly.

He presented the task to the members of his court, but the next day, the king saw through the palace window that the bird had still not moved from its perch.

Having tried everything else, the king thought to himself, "Maybe I need someone more familiar with the countryside to understand the nature of this problem." So he cried out to his court, "Go and get a farmer."

In the morning, the king was thrilled to see the falcon soaring high above the palace gardens. He said to his court, "Bring me the doer of this miracle."

The court quickly located the farmer, who came and stood before the king. The king asked him, "How did you make the falcon fly?"

With his head bowed, the farmer said to the king, "It was very easy, your highness. I simply cut the branch where the bird was sitting."

To realize our incredible potential, we often go through a plethora of negative situations which have ways of testing our personal resolve. Our comfort zone is on the branch of life where we are content and at ease until we are moved by situations that force us to reposition ourselves. When our tree of comfort is shaken by disappointment and failure, we are faced with a question of "What now?" Do we continue to find another comfort branch, or do we soar and live on the zenith of life's mountain?

Walt Disney, the creator and founder of the Disney empire, did not start with this glamorous story of success. In fact, it was just the opposite. Today, Disney rakes in billions of dollars from merchandise, movies, and theme parks around the world, but Walt Disney himself had a bit of a rough start.

The Failures of the Successful

He was fired by a newspaper editor who said, "Walt lacked imagination and had no good ideas." After that, Walt Disney started a number of businesses that didn't last long and that ended in bankruptcy. However, he did what very few people do after experiencing a setback. He kept plugging along and eventually found a recipe for success. The wonderful thing about his story is that the very thing the newspaper editor said Disney lacked was what he succeeded at. His imagination and creative idea to draw a friendly mouse in shoes and shorts became the starting point for some of the most lucrative concepts to this day.

Unsuccessful people do not have a corner on the market for failures; in fact, just as much can be learned about failures from a successful person as from an unsuccessful one. Both are intimate with failure—one just decided to stay that way. Unsuccessful people usually miss one great opportunity after another, and this blindness occurs because they see new opportunities as work already done.

When failure becomes your lifestyle, your opinions will reflect it. Opinions are empty of experience but full of unwarranted advice. In fact, experience is nothing more than a collection of events that a person lived through. Successful people aren't interested in fairy tales; they would rather hear real-life stories that shake up familiar paradigms. Gossip and unfounded opinions are child's play; the daily news about Hollywood and "mystery" murders is nothing but a distraction for them. Please don't get me wrong. I am not suggesting that successful people do not enjoy a good movie every now and again, but what I am saying is when it comes to real-life situations, they are not interested in escaping into a movie theater to avoid tackling life or business challenges.

It always amazes me how people come to reflect the attitude of those they meet in the beauty salons and the barber shops. These people, who sit waiting for their appointments, seem passionate about a particular subject, but ask them about their personal experience in the matter, and they have none. This lets me know that their opinions are backed by feelings, not true experience. Usually, strongly opinionated people are those who have never dared to attempt the things they are giving their opinions on.

Failure is not measuring up to your potential. Failure is avoiding risk and playing it safe by working a job instead when living your dream business is what you really desire to do. Failure is when you know you should have had your degree by now, but you dropped out because you were doped up. Failure is when you are making the right amount of money, but you continue to make choices that keep you financially broke. Failure is when you are spending money in stores that you should only look through the window of. It doesn't mean that you are going to remain here; it's just that at the present moment, this is where you live.

It is no one's fault but yours when your life is falling apart financially or your low self-esteem is interfering with your marriage because you are personally dissatisfied with your appearance, your weight, etc. Don't get mad at the world; no one lives in your body but you.

There is a system of success and a system of failure. It has been said that success is a journey; but I say so is failure. And just as success is a mindset, failure also is a mindset. Success is an attitude; failure is an attitude. Most people are rich in attitude, but lacking in experience. Many people have a lot to say about everything, but no experience in anything. What is even worse is that they actually have an audience. No wonder most people are in the same boat.

I often say that I would rather listen to Peter (Jesus' disciple), who got out of the boat and walked on water, though he ultimately failed, than listen to the eleven other disciples who stayed in the boat because they were too afraid to fail. All that the eleven disciples

The Failures of the Successful

could give you is an opinion about what Peter should have done, but they had no experience of what should have been done. It's funny that the people who attempt to do nothing are always offering advice to the people who are doing something.

If you have never organized and operated as much as a Kool-Aid stand, you are in no position to instruct the person who has a business on how they should run their business. If these adventurous, successful people want your advice on a matter, I'm sure they will hand you a comment card. Opinions are oftentimes unsolicited advice. Start your own Kool-Aid stand, and then you will be able to pack real experience into your opinion. Until then, keep your opinions to yourself. If you won't listen to your own advice, why should others? Nothing becomes real or indisputable until it is experienced.

Opinions, as I have defined them, are usually not attached to experience, so be careful whose opinion you value. Most people spend their lives compensating for failure, and yet have become self-appointed experts in fields they have never been exposed to. If you fail continually, it is evident that you have adopted a system of failure. You have become experienced in failure, but you disguise your failure by giving your opinions on matters where you have no experience.

Oftentimes, people give their opinions to make themselves appear successful in the eyes of other failures. Stop pretending! The battle to succeed is ultimately you against yourself, not you against your opposition. The voice in your mind telling you that you cannot succeed against the odds is what you must defeat. Silence the voice of failure by succeeding at what you have previously failed to accomplish. Don't stop at your attempt until you succeed.

One of the most damaging lies you hear is the one you tell yourself. The lie your mind creates that causes you to think that you are fighting against someone or something else. Success doesn't always go to the most talented, the strongest, or the most scholarly person, but rather to the person who can silence that small voice of self-doubt and beat out his or her personal best. Believe me; I know what it feels like when you come face to face with your own inadequacies.

I can recall a situation that I personally wanted to avoid facing because I lived under this lie for so long that my financial circumstances were not necessarily all my own fault. I was watching a particular episode of Dave Ramsey talking on the subject of personal finances. I must admit that I was getting pretty angry as I heard Dave speak on controlling spending and avoid by buying unnecessary items and addressing the real problem inside of why you need such things, especially when you cannot afford them. It felt as if Dave was speaking directly to me while pointing his finger in my face. Even though there were other disparaging things mentioned by Dave, I could not justify sitting there trying to rationalize my financial situation. The truth of the matter was that I was deeply in debt with an income that had hit its ceiling. Dave was right, and I decided then not to become angry at the wrong person. Dave Ramsey was not my enemy, I was my own enemy. The moment I accepted the truth about my financial debt was the moment a whole new world opened up to me. I buckled down and wrote down my liabilities and assets and started to work on paying my debts off. I was able to create other revenue sources all because my mentality shifted from liability oriented to asset-oriented.

My good friend Mark Victor Hansen and his partner, Jack Canfield, collaborated on the first *Chicken Soup for the Soul* book, compiling inspirational, true stories they had heard. Many of these stories came from people who attended their motivational conferences. Their book was initially rejected by major publishers in New York and seemingly every publisher's door they knocked on remained closed, until they stumbled onto a small self-help publisher in Florida, called HCI, who accepted their book and helped launch the *Chicken Soup for the Soul* series. Mark shared with me the struggles of getting their book published, and he was very clear that it was not a piece of cake. Mark knows firsthand how it feels to continue to have doors closed in his face and yet to find the strength to knock on the next door—until someone finally opens the door.

Don't judge the many who are successful today solely by their success, as though they understand nothing about struggles and failures. Their successes came despite their failures and struggles!

CHAPTER TWENTY-NINE

THE ILLUSION OF GREENER GRASS

"People often ask me whether I prefer theater or film, and the answer is that I prefer the one I'm not doing: The grass is always greener."
—HELEN MIRREN

It always looks greener on the other side because the project you are working on appears to be more stressful than the ones other people are working on.

THERE ONCE WAS A business executive who was deep in debt and could see no way out. Creditors were closing in on him. Suppliers were demanding payment. He sat on a park bench, head in hands, wondering if anything could save his company from bankruptcy. Suddenly an old man appeared before him.

"Young man, I can see something is troubling you," he said. After listening to the executive's woes, the old man said, "I believe I can help you."

The old man asked the man his name, wrote out a check, and pushed it into his hand, saying, "Take this money. Meet me here exactly one year from today, and you can pay me back at that time." Then he turned and disappeared as quickly as he had come.

The business executive saw in his hand a check for $500,000, signed by John D. Rockefeller—one of the richest men in the world!

"I can erase my money worries in an instant!" he realized. The executive decided not to cash the check, but to put it in his safe. Just knowing it was there gave him the strength to work out a way to save his business. With renewed optimism, he negotiated better deals and extended terms of payment. He closed several big sales. Within a few months, he was out of debt and making money once again.

Exactly one year later, he returned to the park with the same check, uncashed. At the agreed-upon time, the old man appeared. But just as the executive was about to hand back the check and share his success story, a nurse came running up and grabbed the old man.

"I'm so glad I caught him!" she cried. "I hope he hasn't been bothering you. He's always escaping from the rest home and telling people he's John D. Rockefeller." She led the old man away by the arm.

The astonished executive just stood there, stunned. All year long he'd been wheeling and dealing, buying and selling, convinced he had half-a-million dollars behind him. Suddenly, he realized it wasn't the money, real or imagined, that had turned his life around. It was his newfound self-confidence that gave him the power to achieve anything he went after.

The Illusion of Greener Grass

In the preceding story, the executive found the courage to get back in the game of business after a huge disappointment. Why was his self-confidence all of a sudden riding high? He had complete confidence in what he thought he possessed. The phony $500,000 check was his placebo, which actually made him dig deeper within himself, become more creative than he had been in the past, and believe more in his ability to get the job done.

People so often play themselves short, assuming they are a failure because someone else's life seems to be better than theirs. If your decision making has gotten you into the mess that now exists, it will be that same decision-making ability, this time with careful consideration, that will exonerate you from the mess you've made.

I once had a conversation with a gentleman who appeared to be in his midthirties and spoke of how unfair he thought this world was to the unfortunate. Obviously, he viewed himself as one of those unfortunate people who never get a break. I could easily pick up his attitude toward people who seem to have it all, because he mentioned how most wealthy people haven't a clue about what it means to ration their food—while staying up and burning the candle on both ends to make a buck.

After hearing this young man voice one displeasure after another, I asked him a question. "Do you know any of these people you're speaking of? You sound like you know some of them very well."

"No, I just know they will never understand what it's like to struggle financially," he said. "If I had their money, I would be just as creative and innovative to increase my bottom line as they are."

The best of us have been on the side of this young man before, thinking the grass is greener on the other side. But it is not net worth that matters most; it is self-worth that is supreme. Your ability is incredible and your knowledge is extensive. Your focus should be on developing you, not on attempting to live your life similarly to the way others are living theirs.

Stop looking at your neighbor's lawn and start taking care of your own by fertilizing it and giving it sufficient water. You will discover your grass is just as green, if not greener. Things may not be going so well right now, but it doesn't mean things will remain the same throughout your lifetime. Situations, circumstances, and problems are all scenarios subject to change. You may not need a miracle to straighten things out in your life; you may only need a little focus, dedication, and belief in your ability to turn things around.

Imagine the power of self-confidence when you believe in yourself. Your qualities are intrinsic and your skill level is without limits. You can stretch yourself as far as you believe you can. Therefore, take a deep breath and plunge into the best YOU ever.

You do not need money in order to have confidence in yourself and your abilities. You can create so much more money and do so much more with your present life. The best investment you can ever make is in yourself. If you will decide to take care of your own grass, you will never be tempted to speak about how much greener the grass looks on the other side. It doesn't matter where you start or how you start—what does matter is how you finish.

I believe the right talk will eventually lead to the right results. The wrong talk will produce the wrong results. The Good Book actually says in Mark 11:24, paraphrased, You shall have whatever you say. In other words, people should be careful of what they say because every time they speak out loud, they are programming themselves and others around them. To speak so favorably of other people's qualities may be admirable, but to discard your own qualities is a disservice to yourself.

The Illusion of Greener Grass

Many people undervalue who and what they are, but what is worse is when people overvalue who they are not. Usually this occurs when people allow criticism to get to their hearts. And, with that, people incarcerate themselves in a prison of fear of what others think of them.

One of the greatest formulas you can discover in life is how to renew your mind by transitioning your thoughts from one form to another—from thought to material, from mindset to heart thoughts. The reality of your world is not what you experience first, but what you envision first. Thoughts are the materials that precede the reality of their creation. If you view situations that confront you as too powerful and strong to overcome, then you will see your future accomplishments as hopeless. There is no condition that is irreversible. All that can be broken is fixable.

To believe is to start, and what you believe has the potential for existence. Life doesn't occur until the stuff in your heart comes out of your mouth—good, bad, or indifferent. I often say, don't speak out of your frustrations because you will have to live with the Frankenstein you verbally create.

Everyone is guilty of taking so much for granted, especially when it comes to the people in their lives. It takes a great deal of spiritual and emotional stability to maintain a sense of contentment with what you have and to be able to resist the temptation of thinking that other people have it better. My mother used to say to me, whenever I brought up what my friends were allowed to do by their parents, "You don't know what goes on behind closed doors."

I discovered how true that statement actually is when I encountered people who put on a good public show about the success of their business, but ended up bankrupt just one year later. Your life may not be easy, but it's your life. The quickest way you can change any condition in your life or business is to make a definitive decision.

Stop admiring your neighbor's lawn, business, house, career, whatever, and start taking care of your own.

⁂

A psychologist walked around a room while teaching stress management to an audience. As she raised a glass of water, everyone expected they'd be asked the "half-empty or half-full" question. Instead, with a smile on her face, she inquired, "How heavy is this glass of water?"

Answers called out ranged from eight ounces to twenty ounces. Finally, she responded. "The absolute weight doesn't matter. It depends on how long I hold it. If I hold it for a minute, it's not a problem. If I hold it for an hour, I'll have an ache in my arm. If I hold it for a day, my arm will feel numb and paralyzed. In each case, the weight of the glass doesn't change, but the longer I hold it, the heavier it becomes."

She continued, "The stresses and worries in life are like this glass of water. Think about them for a while and nothing happens. Think about them a bit longer and they begin to hurt. And if you think about them all day long, you will feel paralyzed—incapable of doing anything."

It's important to remember to let go of your stresses, especially when your concerns are about keeping up with the Joneses. Don't invest your attention in something so trivial; time costs too much to waste.

For the sake of argument, let us assume for a moment that other people's lives and situations are much better than yours. How do you know their situations will remain the same? Situations and circumstances are always changing. A person can be up one moment and down the next. That applies to business, marriages, careers, and whatever else you would like to put on the list.

What matters most, right at this moment, is what you have and who you are. Cultivate what you have, develop who you are, and watch things change in your life. What will it take for you to notice and appreciate the gifts and talents you have?

Throughout my years, I have heard some great stories of peoples' awakening moments. There's a story of a grandmother who was dying. She spoke to her grandson, Joshua, about his future, and although he loved his grandmother dearly, he wanted no part of the family business. He didn't want to go back to college, and he still found himself experimenting with drugs. In her final moments, she motioned for her grandson to come near.

"You have a lot of good qualities in you, son," she said. "Your grandfather and your dad never stopped believing in you. I am the last of the family business, and I cannot run our business from this bed. Son, don't disappoint your children; they are depending on you to leave a legacy for them."

After his grandmother passed, Joshua couldn't help but wonder why she would talk about his children when he had none at the time. He was only twenty-four and had no plans for children. In fact, he had no plans at the moment to even enter into a serious relationship.

Two weeks after the funeral, he met the most beautiful girl he'd ever laid eyes on, Jess. He entreated her, and they seemed to hit it off. Jess spoke of her father getting diagnosed with cancer and of how his doctor had given him one year to live. She informed

Joshua how she did not feel qualified to run her father's business. Joshua quickly interrupted and spoke of how he didn't want any part of his family's business.

"Why are you so angry?" she asked. "I'm sure that your family only wants the best for you."

"They just want me to follow the plans they have for me. But I have my own plans," he exclaimed.

She sat in thought for a moment, then began collecting her things.

"I have to go," she said.

"Can I see you again?" Joshua asked.

"I don't know. I have no room for anyone in my life right now because I am trying to finish school."

Joshua was curious and asked, "What school do you attend?" Her answer was the same university he once attended, dropping out with just one class to complete to receive his bachelor of science in Business degree.

They ended up spending much of the next week together, and he became inspired to go back to school, graduating with his degree. Joshua didn't realize how much his plans had changed by meeting this young beautiful woman, but he knew that he didn't want to spend the rest of his life without her.

Six months later, he took over his family's business and asked Jess to marry him. Joshua and Jess were a match made in heaven. While he was growing in family, so was his business. He accelerated the company's growth by implementing new creative ideas and was able to increase the company's revenue by 330 percent. However, even as his business was flourishing, Jess' father's business was failing under the guidance of her older brother.

One day, Joshua's father's best friend came to visit him, as he periodically would. They talked for a while, and Joshua said that his father always seemed to know what he wanted to do and that he had handled the business so well.

"That wasn't always the case," his father's friend said. "Your dad wanted to have nothing to do with your family's business. When your great grandmother was dying, she spoke to your father and said, 'Son, you have a lot of good qualities in you. Your grandfather and your dad never stopped believing in you and neither have I. Your father cannot run our business with degenerative arthritis, and I cannot run it from this bed. Son, don't disappoint your children; they are depending on you to leave a legacy for them.'"

Joshua sobbed. Those were the exact words his grandmother had said to him. He suddenly knew what he had to do with what he had always hidden in his heart for their business. He took over his father-in-law's business, joined the two companies together, and grew the company to the value of over $200 million.

How to Avoid the Green Grass Syndrome

Let me give you three quick points that will help you avoid the green grass syndrome. This is not to say that these points will cause you to avoid being delusional, but they will help you to detect illusions in your life. An illusion is something that deceives by producing a false or misleading impression of reality. Life is not a one-size-fits-all scenario. What may be good for one person may not be good for you, and learning to detect these illusions is the first step to taking care of your own grass.

1. Your life is the only life you have. You cannot transfer into someone else's body and live their life. In fact, putting your brain in another person's body will not fix anything because the same thought pattern is there, just in a different body. Your self-esteem may spike temporarily, but the

first insult that bruises you will result in the same problem you had in your old body. It's your body, your mind, and your life—enjoy it.
2. Strongly consider your spouse and the years the two of you have spent together. The secret to staying in love is maintaining a fresh mental video, remembering how you felt when you first knew you were in love. Love doesn't change, people do. Love is constant, people are inconsistent. The out-of-shape body, the wrinkles on the face, and the slow decline of health are all symptoms of the body, but not the soul of the person. We all will grow older; however, make a decision not to grow old.
3. Business and how business is done always fluctuates. Staying on top of the latest marketing schemes and improving your connectivity with your client base are the keys to staying focused in this unstable economy. When you become lethargic in your efforts and your zeal has been replaced with apathy, of course, it's going to affect your business.

How do you distract a man with a dream? Give him another dream. You cannot chase two rabbits at the same time or you will end up losing both of them. You grow as you learn; and when you learn more, you earn more. If business is down, the right ingredients and effort will cause it to start climbing again.

If you worry about what might be, and wonder what might have been, you will ignore what is. If your business is not doing well financially, you already know that it isn't. If you know how your business arrived to this point, you are already aware of that as well. So the next step is not to consider the past, nor the present, but the future. Give no attention to what is—instead, give attention to what you want to be.

CHAPTER THIRTY

The Strength of Perseverance

"I do not think that there is any other quality as essential
to success of any kind as the quality of perseverance.
It overcomes almost everything, even nature."
—John D. Rockefeller

*Life may not have promised you a rose garden, but its principles
do suggest that you can have a rose garden if you plant one. To
make it in this life is to tune out the ones who believe they can't.*

There once was a bunch of tiny frogs who arranged a climbing competition. The goal was to reach the top of a very high tower. A big crowd had gathered around the tower to see the race and cheer on the contestants, even though no one really believed that the tiny frogs would reach the top of the tower. As the race began, the crowd kept making comments like "Oh, this is way too difficult!" and "They will never make it to the top," and "Not a chance they'll succeed. The tower is too high!"

Turn on Your Life

Indeed, the tiny frogs began collapsing one by one—except for a few who in a fresh tempo were climbing higher and higher.

The crowd continued to yell, "It is too difficult! No one will make it!"

More tiny frogs got tired and gave up, but one continued climbing higher and higher and higher. This one tiny frog wouldn't give up! At the end, this frog was the only one who, after a big effort, reached the top.

Of course, all of the other tiny frogs wanted to know how this one frog managed it. A contestant asked the tiny frog how he had succeeded in finding the strength to reach the goal. It turned out . . . that the winner was deaf.

The secret to making it through life successfully is learning to shut out the voices that are telling you that you can't make it. Although it is difficult to not pay attention to the loud voices of naysayers, if you are paying attention to them, you are already paying too much.

If I could give, in a single word, the ingredient that people lack in the pursuit of their goals, it would be perseverance. Perseverance, in its most generic term, is the ability to "keep on keeping on." Most people have no idea how critical this word is to their success.

How do you continue doing the things that you have committed yourself to doing when there seems to be no fruit production from your labor? How do you continue doing something when you no longer like doing it?

This matter of perseverance is so critical to life that above all human traits, the perseverance characteristic should be built into the psyche and life of every child. The Greek word for perseverance literally means "staying power." The ability to remain focused under

The Strength of Perseverance

pressure is key while traveling on the road of success. If success is a journey, then perseverance is the vehicle used en route. While you are traveling on any road, there will be some bumps (disappointments) and potholes (obstacles) that you must learn to avoid.

It is easy to start the race with exuberance, but it is not so easy to finish. Every marriage starts with the blissful thought of a couple being together forever, but today approximately 60 percent of them end in divorce. All dreamers start off with the idea that their business concept is the best on the market and that they are going to be on the fast track to sell tons of their products, only to end up disappointed.

What happened with a marriage that ends in divorce? This question is easy; rather than preparing for forty or even sixty years, which takes work, people who get divorced think that the marriage will take care of itself, and they make no preparations at all. This is why we have such great starters out from the gates, but very few ever make it to the finish line. They end up making some lame excuses so that they do not look bad in the eyes of their contemporaries. But what does it matter what other people think when you yourself realize that you didn't fail because you did not have the right stuff, but that you failed because you quit?

The opposite of perseverance is giving up. I personally know what it feels like to be in a hard place in life, as if you are in a dark tunnel, traveling for days with no light in sight. It can be hard to concentrate when the darkness literally impedes your view. However, making the conscious decision to move forward is a matter of knowing what you want and how bad you want it. Being faced with turbulent times tests your faith, stretches your resilience, and brings your toughness into question. I know, I know . . . no one likes to be in this place; but everyone ends up there at some point. What each person has to decide in a situation that seems to have no visible options is does the dream go on, does the marriage go on, and does the business go on?

Get inspired! Get turned on! Never, never quit because you will never get to see what the end will actually look like. Your dream is worth the fight, and so is your life. Hold on and keep on keeping on.

CHAPTER THIRTY-ONE

True Expectations

"Don't lower your expectations to meet your
performance. Raise your level of performance to meet
your expectations. Expect the best of yourself, and
then do what is necessary to make it a reality."
—Ralph Marston

*Most people do not have a problem with having expectations;
their problem is in what their expectations are.*

NOTHING GIVES A PERSON HOPE like having an expectation. In fact, expectation is the anticipation that the probability of something happening is greater than the probability of it not happening. The unfortunate thing about expectation is that it doesn't make things happen—it looks for things to happen. This position of expectation usually places a person in an interim between reality and expectation. And, when reality is viewed as permanent, expectations are usually pointless. It is, therefore, absolutely essential that you understand the underlying principle of having an expectation.

I am not saying that people should not have expectations. There is nothing quite like expectation to give people a sense of hope. Expectation gives people the motivation to look up instead of looking down, as if all hope is gone. It is the gap between the reality of where people are and the expectation to be where they want to go. When expectations are not met, it is easy for people to become discouraged. William Shakespeare said, "Expectation is the root of all heartache." This sounds more like disappointment to me.

My advice is to view your expectations not as something that you simply want to achieve, but as a shifting of realities. As discussed previously, realities are not permanent because everything is subject to change. Everything is the way it is because each person has agreed that that is the way it is. However, it doesn't have to be that way for you. Expectation has everything to do with your internal system of belief. Physical reality is that which when you stop believing in it, doesn't go away. Therefore, your reality versus your expectation is actually your present life (present reality) versus your future life (expected reality).

So, how should you view your expectations? I'm glad you asked. People often only view expectation as something that provides them the room to stretch and grow; it becomes the height of their ceiling. However, it can also become their floor to move lower. Expectations are not always what people may aspire to achieve; they can also be whatever low levels people fear to fall to.

My suggestions are to set your expectations to reach higher without the mental apprehensions of perhaps the opposite. For example: You may have a mental picture of being healthier and feeling more energetic by losing those extra forty pounds you have been carrying for the last ten years. You may also have the thought in the back of your mind of losing some of the weight but gaining back more pounds than what you lost. This too is an expectation. One expectation is conscious, and the other is subconscious. Both of your expectations are real, but only one of them goes to the core of your belief.

At your present moment, you are what you subconsciously believe. As you start to shift the thoughts of your frontal brain to the rear, to your subconscious mind, you will shift your entire life from what you want to achieve to what you believe you can achieve.

Understand that there will be an internal conflict because you are moving a surface belief to a deep core belief, and this does not happen without combat. It is a fight; however, it is possible to win. Once you change your core beliefs to match what you truly want, you can't help but to be what you think. As a man thinks in his heart, so is he.

Notice that a man is what he thinks in his heart, not what he thinks in his head. Your brain may cause you to say something different than what you truly believe, but your heart will trigger the reactionary process to act out what you in reality believe. Everyone has, at one time or another, spoken words contrary to how they act because they didn't like what they did. It's like the thief who doesn't see himself as one. His mind causes the mouth to speak what is not true sometimes, but he will eventually do what he is predisposed to doing because of what's in his heart—his core belief. Thus, he acts only on what he is, not what he wants to be.

To believe is an expectation, not a reservation. You have the power to change your world and to change what you do! Is that so hard to believe? Because what you cannot retain in your heart of hearts, you cannot possess in your life. The person who expects by faith will also be transformed by it. In other words, you live by and in what changed you.

It is impossible to play a violin with broken strings. Similarly, you cannot make your heart feel what it doesn't believe, and therefore, no one can convince you of anything that isn't first real to you. The beginning of every champion begins in the heart of the person. A great expected future that does not begin today will remain an illusion or an esoteric impenetrable consciousness. You will either believe in your circumstances or believe that you can change them.

Your world of material form simply reflects what is going on in your thinking. Your future is not given to chance—it's given to you. You begin to form your expected future by the decisions you make today. Beyond the world you see and are now experiencing is the world you really desire to excavate and live in.

I started one of my companies with a dream and a prayer. I didn't have all the money I needed—in fact, I had very little liquidity—but my expectation was to succeed and not fail. I wasn't afraid to do what was unconventional. I saw my vision as clear as day, and I believed that this would be a way to not only provide employment for people, but to serve as a little piece of home for those in the military. Needless to say, our restaurant opened on time on a military installation, providing home-cooked, delicious food that could remind most soldiers of mom's cooking. And just to think, it all started with a dream and a prayer.

Understand that deep within your hope is the possibility of your expectations being attained. Choose hope over fear.

CHAPTER THIRTY-TWO
UPGRADE YOUR LIFE (STYLE)

"I don't want to get to the end of my life and find that I lived just the length of it. I want to have lived the width of it as well."
—Diane Ackerman

Achieving the life you desire has nothing to do with hard work; it has to do with working smart and knowing that not only do you deserve it, you demand it.

An American businessman was standing at the pier of a small coastal Mexican village when a small boat with just one fisherman docked. Inside the small boat were several large yellowfin tunas. The American complimented the Mexican on the quality of his fish.

"How long did it take you to catch them?" the American asked.

"Ah, only a little while," the Mexican replied.

"Why don't you stay out longer and catch more fish?" the American asked.

"I have enough to support my family's immediate needs," the Mexican said.

"But," the American said, "what do you do with the rest of your time?"

"I sleep late, fish a little, play with my children, take a siesta with my wife, Maria, stroll into the village each evening where I sip wine and play guitar with my amigos. I have a full and busy life, señor."

The American scoffed. "I am a Harvard MBA and could help you. You should spend more time fishing, and with the proceeds you could buy a bigger boat, and with the proceeds from the bigger boat, you could buy several boats. Eventually you would have a fleet of fishing boats. Instead of selling your catch to a middleman, you would sell directly to the consumers, eventually opening your own can factory. You would control the product, processing, and distribution. You would need to leave this small village and move to Mexico City, then Los Angeles, and eventually New York City, where you will run your expanding enterprise."

"But, señor, how long will this all take?" the Mexican asked.

"Fifteen to twenty years," the American replied.

"But what then, señor?"

The American laughed. "That's the best part. When the time is right, you would announce an IPO—an initial public offering—and sell your company stock to the public and become very rich. You would make millions."

"Millions, señor? Then what?"

The American said slowly: "Then you would retire. Move to a small coastal fishing village where you would sleep late, fish a little, play with your kids, take a siesta with your wife, stroll to the village in the evenings where you could sip wine and play your guitar with your amigos . . ."

Upgrade Your Life (Style)

Are you overscheduled and underrested? Are you searching for ways to improve your life? Do you believe that what you have experienced to this day is all there is to life? There is so much more life locked inside of you that it would be an absolute travesty to settle at where you are. Personal fulfillment comes from having no regrets at the end of the day because you believe you made the right decisions. This doesn't mean that you stop here as if the next day is automatically filled with the accomplishments of yesterday—yesterday's actions just get you closer to meeting your goal today.

Stop wasting your time attempting things that have nothing to do with your personal passion. Doing what everyone else does is not how life is supposed to be. You have to reach for your own star, live your own dream, and mentally prepare yourself for when you have reached the pinnacle of your accomplishment. I know you have questions that you feel are complicated, but there are simple answers. Sometimes people block their success because they expect something to be complicated. They discard success because they don't recognize a solution in something so simple. It happens all the time . . . well-educated, intelligent, midlife professionals come to realize that their lives need a big change, but they struggle with the answer. The pathway to insightful living reveals answers that are hiding in plain sight for every area of life. From developing a better marital relationship to improving your career options, from a healthy body to healthy finances, life can be upgraded by making the simple decisions that alter your life in powerful ways.

By looking for the insights your mind has to offer, then translating them into clear language and practical actions, you can experience an inner serenity that you might not have believed was even possible. Don't downsize your life because of past failures.

Turn on Your Life

The simplest answer to upgrading your life is discovered in the new choices you can make now.

Change is inevitable, growth is optional. Just because something didn't work out the way you planned it doesn't mean that it wasn't meant to be. It could very well point to the wrong timing rather than the wrong action. You can't preempt certain things because you want them to occur now. Patience has its virtue. You can no more force an orange tree to grow in Alaska than you can make a cherry tree bloom in the fall. Some things are set on a time clock, such as winter, spring, summer, and fall; until you are able to forecast your particular season of change, continue doing what you're doing.

Many people have this notion that a few personal problems are precursors to how bad their lives actually are or are going to be. They often see one problem as a major life crisis, instead of viewing it as a minor inconvenience in need of a simple adjustment. Ultimately, the only person who gets hurt by change is the person who doesn't want to change.

Major problems often need only minor adjustments. It is better for the individual to decide the change they need to make for the better than for the circumstances to force a change they really don't want for the worse.

You are the only person you have been waiting for. To improve your life doesn't call for supplementary things you believe will add the kind of quality to your life that you have been searching for. It is not necessary for you to buy a new car, nor do you have to move into a mansion to feel better about yourself. You are the change that you seek because you know exactly what you want the new you to look like. Yes, these things have their place; but the only value they can add is to your net worth, not your self-worth.

Turn on your life light and get on the fast track to personal growth. Let others know that somebody's home, and you're living life instead of dying. When you commit to upgrading your life, you will be challenged to explore new frontiers and learn skills you never thought you could in a rapidly changing society. Make a large investment in yourself. Pull all your energy together and go for it. The rewards for both personal and professional success are immeasurable. Don't settle for satisfactory when you can upgrade to sensational.

While so many people are downsizing their lives, you must remember that self-worth can never truly be evaluated by mistakes or success. If you are in a business, working a job, or pursuing a career, don't think that achieving the impossible is impossible. Instead of lowering your value to compete with others scraping the bottom of the barrel, raise the value of your life and abilities so that they're irresistible to anyone who encounters you. Always make value, not performance, your main priority.

CHAPTER THIRTY-THREE
Wisdom for a Better Life

"It requires wisdom to understand wisdom: the music is nothing if the audience is deaf."
—Walter Lippmann

People seek knowledge but crave wisdom. Knowledge is more common and easily accessible, but wisdom is uncommon and hard to find because it is only discovered when used.

A WISE PROFESSOR stood before his philosophy class with several items in front of him. As the students quieted down, he picked up a very large and empty jar and proceeded to fill it with golf balls. He then asked the students if the jar was full. They agreed that it was. So the professor then picked up a box of small pebbles and poured them into the jar. He shook the jar lightly. The pebbles rolled into the open areas between the golf balls. He asked the students again if the jar was full. They agreed it was.

The professor next picked up a box of sand and poured it into the jar. Of course, the sand filled up everything else. He asked once more if the jar was full. The students responded with a unanimous "yes." The professor then produced a container of beer from under the table and poured the entire contents into the jar, effectively filling the empty space between the sand. The students laughed.

"Now," said the professor, as the laughter subsided, "I want you to recognize that this jar represents your life. The golf balls are the important things—your family, your children, your health, your friends, your favorite passions—things that, if everything else was lost and only they remained, your life would still be full. The pebbles are the other things that matter like your job, your house, your car.

"The sand is everything else—the small stuff. If you put the sand into the jar first, there is no room for the pebbles or the golf balls. The same goes for life. If you spend all your time and energy on the small stuff, you will never have room for the things that are important to you. Pay attention to the things that are critical to your happiness. Play with your children. Take time to get medical checkups. Take your partner out to dinner. There will always be time to clean the house and fix the rubbish. Take care of the golf balls first, the things that really matter. Set your priorities. The rest is just sand."

One of the students raised her hand and inquired what the beer represented. The professor smiled. "I'm glad you asked. It just goes to show you that, no matter how full your life may seem, there's always room for a cold glass of beer."

Do you know why most people fail to succeed in life? It's not because their goals are entirely *too* lofty and they end up as underachievers; they make goals that are far too easy, and that makes them underachievers. They realize that they can achieve these goals in the dark with their eyes closed; they become comfortable with low risk or no risk, thus eliminating actual challenges.

Those afraid of challenges will never climb the apple tree for the juiciest apples. Instead they will remain on the ground to pick up the apples that fall from the tree. The reality is that many people don't aim at anything for fear that they might fail. Tasting the bitterness from coming up short of reaching your goal should develop in you the hunger to eat the fruit of success.

Choose not to walk by fear; always do more than you think you can do—living by faith has you doing what you believe you can do without you ever having done it before. Worrying about failure or making mistakes causes people to fail and make mistakes. There is a difference between making a mistake and being one. Wisdom will help you calculate the possibilities that come from your choices in order to make the best decisions for your life.

There are three basic reasons why most people rarely reach the pinnacle of enjoying their lives. It's not that these people cannot achieve it; they are simply missing the spoon that stirs the ingredients to create the synergy to make it all happen. These three reasons are:

1. They never had anyone to teach them how to succeed. (Being without a mentor to instruct and encourage you to do more is like traveling through life without a compass.)
2. They never listened to anyone who could help them succeed. (Being educated is the proof that you've learned to listen without being cocky with what you really didn't know.)
3. They never believed that they could succeed. (No person can truly succeed in life without a reasonable sense of confidence to believe one can.)

WISDOM PERSONIFIES LEADERSHIP AND RELATIONSHIPS

Have you ever heard the phrase, "It's lonely at the top"? I believe God intended for leaders to lead from a place of seclusion, not inclusion. Leaders need to be alone with their thoughts to strategize how to be more productive and less destructive. Leaders don't mind being unpopular when necessary.

Wisdom can help people to read developing relationships and if they are worth engaging in. There are two kinds of relationships: nourishing and toxic. Nourishing relationships bring the best out of people while at the same time making them more productive and audacious, inspiring them to reach peak levels. Toxic relationships are poisonous and fatal to success. These relationships drain people of their creativity and mislead them down paths of no return.

Ask yourself this question about the people around you: What is this relationship doing to me? What am I receiving out of this relationship? Is it making me better or bitter toward others? Am I inspired to dream or do I want to watch television all day? Am I becoming more of a person of character or less than a person of character?

There is a psychology term called "relational illness" that applies directly to these relational scenarios. Relational illness is an uncontrollable problem that exists between at least two people, affecting how they communicate with each other. The people aren't bad in and of themselves, it's just that the relating to each other is incomprehensible. Some people are making you sick and unproductive, and you are blind to it. You cannot change these people, and it is an around-the-clock job even trying. It is better to rid yourself of them.

CAN WISDOM LEAD ME TO A BETTER LIFE?

Wisdom is important if you want to not just be happy, but to stay happy. Wisdom is not an esoteric, elusive characteristic that only the rich and famous or university professors or some old religious person can attain. Anyone can have wisdom if it is sought over knowledge. A person doesn't have to necessarily know how to conjugate a verb in order to be wise. The smartest among us can be the most ignorant in simple matters. In fact, smart people have made horrible decisions about their lives. It takes more than book-smart knowledge to attain a better life—it literally involves intangibles that must be accepted and believed in.

Can wisdom help better your life? Yes—a resounding yes! One of the reasons wisdom will unequivocally help your life to be more fluent and productive is that it will help you hone in on two basic principles and beliefs: it will help you identify who you are, and it will help you to not only know what you believe, but also to define what you believe.

If you are going to live, you might as well live life to its fullest. This should not be pursued with reckless abandon. No one should set out to conquer the world without first conquering oneself. Bad habits, insatiable appetites, and out-of-control behavior might seem like fun at first, but the fun will soon subside. These horrible qualities will drain your life of the excitement of just being alive. Why would anyone want to live out of control? Doing whatever you want to do in the moment will lead to regret, but consciously making sound choices to do what will benefit and enrich your life is commendable.

There was once a young man who started his career after college to change the world, but he noticed that as he went overseas to other countries how difficult it was because of the language barriers. So he decided to change his country, but he found it difficult to narrow down an audience. Not discouraged, he started out to change his state, but no one would listen to him. The young man's aspirations appeared to be failing, so he changed his strategy and went out to change his city and community, but they considered him a youth who needed more experience. However, when the young man made a conscious decision to change himself, he became happy with himself. His attitude was so infectious that people were drawn to him—and without noticing what had transpired, he became instrumental in changing his community, then his city, his state, his country, and then he conquered the world. As a young man with simple ideas, he ended up a billionaire and later died. That man was Steve Jobs. This is his story in a nutshell.

Your life means something—and wisdom will help you discover it. GET PUMPED—YOU'RE ALIVE!

Wisdom will help you discover solutions to life problems, business woes, and relationship challenges.

Problems and solutions are both neutral within our orb of existence and are only engendered when choices are made. However, if life seems to be problematic, then it must have had a creator to instigate its reality. The problem and the solution are one in the same because they are both created from the same substance. A problem originates as a result of the bad decisions or choices made which ignited the problem to materialize. Oftentimes, critical thinking must be applied in order to see the solution which hides in the crevasses of the problem. Norman Vincent Peale said, "Every problem has in it the seeds of its own solution. If you don't have any problems, you don't get any seeds."

When an individual creates their own difficulty and tries to get others to repair it, it only exacerbates the problems. Solutions can be so easily discovered if a person would only go backward to the place before the problem began, to reconsider the choices which were made. Allowing others to come into the middle of your situation, to help bring a resolution to your concerns without understanding the origin of it, will be of no real significance to you. It's so much easier to suggest solutions when you don't know too much about the problem. Think about it, when the government tries to fix problems with private corporations, the government's solutions to their problems are usually as bad as the problems themselves; because the symptoms get the attention, not the problems.

True visionary people face the same problems everyone else faces. The only difference with the visionary is rather than becoming paralyzed by the problem, they immediately commit themselves to finding a solution by investigating the mechanics of that particular problem. Although some level of stress may exist within them, especially when there are time restraints to consider, they refuse to seek relief from the stress because they realize their focus will be misdirected away from finding the solution.

Let me quickly define the word 'problem,' because it may clear up some misconceptions you may have about a problem. A problem is something which is difficult to deal with, or it is difficulty understanding something or a source of trouble with the potential to result in anxiety. However, a 'solution' is defined as something used or done to deal with and end a problem, something which solves a problem or the condition of being solved.

Not everything or everyone you consider a problem, actually exists as one. Some occurrences or people are only problems because this is the way a person may see them. A solution is like connecting the dots, which points to the answer. Some solutions may seem difficult, but not impossible to implement.

For instance, eating is not the problem for people who are overweight; however, what you eat and how much of it can be the problem to obesity. Changing what is eaten and how much is consumed is the solution to one's overweight condition. So, within the same context of eating as a problem, eating is also the solution—considering one governs their intake.

What if a person has money concerns? Like the problem with overindulgence of food, losing the excess weight is going to be a process. The only solution to money problems is money. The solution is not in having more money; the solution is in managing the money you have. You see, the solution is hidden in the problem itself. Finding a job paying twice the amount you are currently making will not answer your money concerns. When a person thinks this way, it is because they have no clue the extra money will only mask the problem and immediately deal with the symptom. But, when the extra money ointment wears off, they will be left with the same age-old problem.

There is no happiness in ignorance. Find your solutions before your problems start a serious revolution.

CHAPTER THIRTY-FOUR
Uncompromised Dedication

> "Confidence doesn't come out of nowhere. It's a result of something . . . hours and days and weeks and years of constant work and dedication."
> —Roger Staubach

The way a person can destroy their own dedication is by listening to the wrong advice.

John was the kind of guy you love to hate, though not in a bad way. He was always in a good mood and always had something positive to say. When someone would ask him how he was doing, he would reply, "If I were any better, I would be twins!" He was a natural motivator. If an employee was having a bad day, John was there telling the employee how to look on the positive side of the situation.

Seeing his way of thinking really made me curious, so one day I went up to John and asked him, "I don't get it. You can't be a positive person all of the time. How do you do it?"

John replied, "Each morning I wake up and say to myself, 'You have two choices today. You can choose to be in a good mood or you can choose to be in a bad mood.' I choose to be in a good mood. Each time something bad happens, I can choose to be a victim or I can choose to learn from it. I choose to learn from it. Every time someone comes to me complaining, I can choose to accept their complaining or I can point out the positive side of life. I choose the positive side of life."

"Yeah, right, it's not that easy," I protested.

"Yes, it is," John said. "Life is all about choices. When you cut away all the junk, every situation is a choice. You choose how you react to situations. You choose how people affect your mood. You choose to be in a good mood or bad mood. The bottom line: It's your choice how you live your life."

I reflected on what John said. Soon after, I left the SOAR Industry to start my own business. We lost touch, but I often thought about him when I decided to choose life instead of reacting to it.

Several years later, I heard that John was involved in a serious accident, falling some fifty feet from a communications tower. After eighteen hours of surgery and weeks of intensive care, John was released from the hospital with rods placed in his back. I saw John about six months after the accident. When I asked him how he was, he replied. "If I were any better, I'd be twins. Would you like to see my scars?"

I declined to see his wounds, but I did ask him what had gone through his mind as the accident took place. "The first thing that went through my mind was the well-being of my soon-to-be-born daughter," John replied. "Then, as I lay on the ground, I remembered that I had two choices: I could choose to live or I could choose to die. I chose to live."

"Weren't you scared? Did you lose consciousness?" I asked.

John continued, "The paramedics were great. They kept telling me I was going to be fine. But when they wheeled me into the ER and I saw the expressions on the faces of the doctors and nurses, I got really scared. In their eyes, I read 'He's a dead man.' I knew I needed to take action."

"What did you do?" I asked.

"Well, there was a burly nurse shouting questions at me," said John. "She asked if I was allergic to anything. 'Yes,' I replied. The doctors and nurses stopped working as they waited for my reply. I took a deep breath and yelled, 'Gravity!' Over their laughter, I told them, 'I am choosing to live. Operate on me as if I am alive, not dead.'"

John lived, thanks to the skill of his doctors, but also because of the amazing attitude that he embodied as a result of his dedication to being a positive person. I learned from him that every day we have the choice to live fully, however, dedication is required.

What is your level of dedication? Is dedication necessary for success? If so, how dedicated should one be if they are going to succeed? Can a person succeed with half-hearted dedication? The answer is yes, if the task before them requires little or no dedication. However, if the challenge is daunting and extremely difficult, which in most cases are the battles worth fighting; it will take everything in a person to succeed.

Dedication can never be categorized as a neutral void in the middle. You are either dedicated or you're not; there is no in-between. Dedication is vital for success in anything you do, but especially in whatever your ultimate life pursuit may be.

I once spoke to a young pastor who was facing discouragement in his first pastoral position because church attendance seemed dismal. He assured me that he wasn't discouraged, but he admitted that he was in one heck of a battle to not capitulate to discouragement. I spoke an analogy to him about the difference between discouragement and encouragement. "How does discouragement look?" I asked. I said, "Discouragement looks like when you've crossed your t's and dotted your i's and have done everything, step-by-step, leaving no stone unturned, and nothing apparently happens. Encouragement looks like when you've crossed your t's and dotted your i's and have done everything, step-by-step, leaving no stone unturned and nothing apparently happens." Both discouragement and encouragement appear as identical twins. However, what separates encouragement from discouragement is your dedication to the task at hand.

To see a business, marriage, or goal through to completion when progress seems to move at a snail's pace means you have to be dedicated so much so that it drives you to stay both motivated and encouraged without losing any enthusiasm in the process.

Dedication is determined by the hours upon hours spent honing in on your craft. A professional athlete understands that the game they play is so competitive, and the margin for error is so slim, that if they are not dedicated to improving themselves to perform at the highest level of their game, they will not last long playing their particular sport. As great as talent is, it is not always enough to succeed. Another person's natural talent may be greater than yours, but their heart and dedication may be diminutive.

I would love to tell you there are shortcuts to succeeding in life, business, or whatever sport you may be presently engaged in, but the truth of the matter is there are none. If success is what you genuinely want in life, it must, not should, be pursued with a phenomenal amount of fortitude and dedication. Don't misunderstand me, winning isn't everything, but it is the most desired outcome for a goal-oriented person, or any competitive athlete who is actually driven to succeed in life or business.

Dedication involves courage, which is the gap between knowing the right thing and doing it. You really don't choose courage and dedication; it chooses you because of your undying devotion to succeed in whatever mandate is laid upon you. It is an empowering decision to stand and fight rather than run, to persevere rather than quit. Dedication is refusing to overlook a difficult challenge standing in your path to prevent you from reaching your goal and choosing to move forward rather than remain stagnate.

What is dedication? It is a very strong mental and emotional support for, or loyalty to, someone or something or a cause. It is not a desire to conquer or rule another person; instead, it is a deep, intrinsic desire to conquer oneself and defeat one's own fears. I believe and have often said people are generally one quality decision away from accomplishing any goal, achieving any personal desire, or obtaining anything they want in life.

Dedication is not only an undying devotion to a particular cause or purpose, but a commitment to thrive and live out one's determination despite the cost. It is not the process of deciding to try or pursue something until it becomes difficult. The person of a dedicated quality mindset, who lives by their personal convictions, is no longer flexible concerning their life assignment; however, they may be flexible concerning their methods. Without preparation and attention to detail, one's actions will not amount to courage. It takes courage and dedication to push through the difficulties of life and to maintain a positive mental attitude. Some people may not understand your relentless drive to do what you do on a daily basis, but they will have to appreciate it.

INDEX

Abraham, 139
action
   beliefs and, 8–9, 64
   impact of one's, 6–7
   intentional, 11–16, 26–7
   words vs., 31–6
Adams, Charles Kendall, 167
adversity. *See* challenges.
advice
   appreciating good, 27
   only as good as giver, 77–8
   wrong, 225
Alexander the Great, 110
Annan, Kofi, 8, 151
anxiety
   ineffectiveness and, 95
   mental sources of, 93
Aristotle, 6
attitude
   choosing powerful, 4–5
   influenced by others, 187–8
   success and, 185–91,
   toward change, 214
Australia, economic conditions in, 156–7

Ball, Lucille, 24
banks, lending practices of, 158
becoming, achievement and, 64
believing in yourself, 62–3, 219.
   See also confidence.
beliefs
   acting in accordance with, 8–9
   displayed in actions, 64
   heart-level, 63–5, 209–10
   restricting, 125–6
   subconscious, 209
Bennett, Bo, 46

boundaries
    beliefs and, 64–5
    motivation to go beyond, 147–50
Boyle, Susan, 14–15
Breedlove, Sarah (Madame C.J. Walker), vii–ix
Brooklyn Bridge, building of, 17–19
Brown, Les, 143
Buffett, Warren, 120, 140, 174
business
    cultivating one's own, 155–60
    fluctuation in, 202
    home-based, 159
    perseverance in, 205–6
    purpose of, 160
    starting one's own, 70, 100–2, 140, 108

California Gold Rush, 129–31
calling, life, 175–6. *See also* life purpose.
Camus, Albert, 153
Cameron, James, 15–16
Canfield, Jack, 190–1
Carey, Mariah, 52–4
Carnegie, Dale, 55, 67
Carson, Dr. Benjamin, 98, 174
Carver, George Washington, 70

challenges
    circumstances viewed as, 94
    facing, 19, 48–52, 135–7, 147–50, 186, 227
    fear of, 219
change, attitude toward, 214
character, business and, 159
charitable giving, 109–10
Churchill, Winston, 4, 83–4
Chicken Soup for the Soul, 190–1
communities, associating with, 27–8, 35 *See also* influence of others.
confidence
    dedication and, 225
    facing challenges and, 49–52
    necessary for success, 219
    power of, 194–7
    pride versus, 168
    self-defeating thoughts and, 84–5
    See also believing in yourself.
connections, choosing, 102–4
consistency, importance of, 63
contentment
    with self, 201–2
    with what one has, 197–9
conviction
    facing challenges and, 48–52
    preference vs., 9

courage, facing challenges and, 43–7, 49–52, 229
Cowell, Simon, 14–15
crises, perspective on, 26
customers, needs of, 160

da Vinci, Leonardo, 152
David and Goliath, story of, 49–52
decision-making ability, 194
decisiveness, importance of, 2, 23–9. *See also* power to decide.
dedication, power of, 225–9
delusions. *See* illusions.
derailment, life, 37–42
discouragement, overcoming, 228
Disney, Walt, 186–7
Doherty, Fraser, 111
Dorsett, Tony, 17
dreams
    necessity of living out, 19–21
    realizing one's, 75–81
Dutton, Charles, 1–2
Dyer, Wayne, 171

economy, business environment and, 156–8
education
    self-education and, 140
    value of, 138, 219

Edison, Thomas, 84
efforts vs. results, 70–3
Emerson, Ralph Waldo, 65, 94
encouragement, 228
escapism, 187
essentials, pursuing first, 137–8

failure
    attitude toward, 185–91
    overcoming, 83–90, 186–7, 215
    perception of, 33
    reasons for, 218–20
    self-esteem and, 188
faith, 64, 116, 219
fate, wealth and, 12. *See also* luck, false value of.
fear
    facing, 45–7. *See also* courage.
    faith vs., 219
    indecisiveness and, 2, 25, 35. *See also* decisiveness.
    self-knowledge and, 144–6
focus
    maintaining, 87–8
    on lucrative projects, 129–133
    on solutions, not problems, 95–6
Ford, Henry, 60
forethought, 25–8

Frankl, Viktor, 3, 5
future, new orientation toward, 113–19

Gates, Bill, vii
Ginóbili, Manu, 147
giving
    creating opportunities through, 109–10
    having before, 137–9
goals
    helping others achieve, 173–4
    setting highest, 171
    setting smaller, 87–8
    too small, 218–19
    wishes vs., 121
God
    limitations and, 64–5
    things already given by, 99
    view of us, 125
government, handling of the economy, 158
gossipers, avoiding, 141–2
greatness, achievement of, 143–6
Green, David, 182
greener grass illusion, 193–202
    steps to avoid, 201–2
Grillparzer, Franz, 97

Hanson, Mark Victor, 174, 190–1
happiness
    choosing, 119–20
    money and, 174–5
heart-level beliefs, 63–5, 209–10
helping others, life purpose and, 173–7
home-based businesses, 159
hope, expectation and, 207–8

Iacocca, Lee, 91
ideas, bank of, 111
illusions, detecting, 201
inadequacies, personal, 190
indecisiveness
    fear and, 2, 25, 35
    too many choices and, 28
individuals, unique value of, 161–5
information, source of, 79–80
influence of others, 27–8, 35, 77–8, 85, 187–8. *See also* communities.
inspiration, 109–10
intrapreneurship, 140–1
investing, 140
Ireland, economic conditions in, 156

James, LeBron, 43, 148
jobs, intrapreneurship and, 140–1
Jobs, Steve, 19–20, 222
Jones, Quincy, 175

Jordan, Michael, 14, 23, 150, 174
Joseph, 141–2
"Joshua," story of, 199–201

Kennedy, John F., 107
King, Dr. Martin Luther, Jr., 170, 176
Kiyosaki, Robert, 185
knowledge
   increase in, 114
   necessary for success, 87
   pursuit of, 104–5
   wisdom and, 104–5, 217, 221
Krause, Jerry, 150

leadership, wisdom and, 220
Lee, Bruce, 181
letting go, 41
life, actively choosing one's, 151–4
life purpose
   finding, 173–7, 179–83, 222
   life goals and, 7–8
   realizing through action, 13–14
limits. *See* boundaries.
Lincoln, Abraham, 173
Lippman, Walter, 217
logic vs. faith, 116
Lombardi, Vince, 147, 167–8, 170

love
   can't live on, 137
   constancy of, 202
luck, false value of, 24. *See also* fate.

Madame Walker Beauty Culturists, viii–ix
Madden, John, 167–8
Malone, Annie Turnbo, viii
Mandela, Nelson, 138, 170
Mandino, Og, 179
marriage
   long-term commitment to, 205–6
   staying in love and, 202
Marshall, James Wilson, 129–31
McWilliams, Lelia, viii
McWilliams, Moses, viii
meaning of life, 137–9
mediocrity, 21, 46, 58, 69, 182
mentors
   finding, 95, 102–4
   guidance from versus following, 168–70
   need for, 219
Meyer, Stephanie, 83–4
miracles, opportunities vs., 108–9
Mirren, Helen, 193
mistakes, perspective on, 57

modesty, false sense of, 120–1
money
    drive to obtain, 139–40
    investing and, 140
    greater purpose of, 183
    happiness and, 174–5
    latent in one's capacities, 65
    love of, 135
    money management and, 100–2
    "tightness" with, 160
    See also wealth-building.
motivation, 17–21, 121, 228

Namath, Joe, 11
naysayers, avoiding, 141–2, 204
Nelson, Dr. Turnel, 151–2
New Year's resolutions, 2
Noah, 123–4
nourishing relationships, 220
NOW (no opportunities wasted), 3–4, 120

obstacles, facing. *See* challenges.
opinions
    reflecting attitude, 187
    unsolicited, 189
opponents, motivation from 147–50
opportunity, acting on, 86–7, 107–11, 120, 142
others, measuring oneself by, 72

Paige, Satchel, 124
past, moving beyond one's, 6, 93, 113–20, 159–60
patience, 85, 149, 214
Paul of Tarsus, 6, 85, 116
peak performance, living at, 13
Peale, Norman Vincent, x, 61, 222
perceptions, responsibility for, 5–6
perfectionism, 87, 149
Perks, Bob, story by, 161–4
Perot, H. Ross, 155
perseverance, 149, 203–6
persistence, 67–70
Peter (apostle), 188–9
planning, success and, 34
possibilities
    beliefs about, 55–60
    unlocking one's personal, 9–10, 143–7
potential
    belief in one's, 9–10, 144–6
    realizing through action, 13–14, 46
Powell, Willie, viii
power to decide, 14–16
preference, conviction vs., 9
present, power of, 3–4
pressure
    managing, 91–6
    techniques for handling, 94–6
pride, self-confidence and, 169

principles, governing action, 13–14
problems, solutions to, ix-xii, 222–4
procrastination
   fear and, 2
   in business, 160

qualities, repression of one's, 97–106
quitting. *See* persistence.

Ramsey, Dave, 190–1
reading, choice of, 78
reality
   perception and, 5–6
   expectations versus, 207–8
Redmoon, Ambrose, 46
regrets, dreams and, 20–21
relational illness, 220
relationships, wisdom and, 220. *See also* marriage.
responsibility, taking full, 35, 94, 135
results. *See* Seven Ordinary Rules for Extraordinary Results.
rewards vs. awards, 71–2
Rockefeller, John D., 203
Roebling, John, 17–18
Roebling, Washington, 18–19
Rohn, Jim, 77, 113, 129
Roosevelt, Eleanor, 24, 69
Rudolph, Wilma, 143
rushing, 94–5

scripture, studying, 35
self-confidence. *See* confidence.
self-control, lack of, 221
self-development, commitment to, 7–8
self-esteem
   career and, 181
   contentment with self and, 201–2
   life purpose and, 8
   overcoming low, 62–3
   overvaluing of self and, 197
   personal empowerment and, 195–6
   self-defeating thoughts and, 84–5
   valuing self and, 215
self-image
   building healthy, 124–5
   self-defeating, 14–15
selfishness, self-development vs., 7
self-knowledge, gaining, 181–2. *See also* life purpose.
self, overvaluing of, 197
self-worth. See self-esteem.
service to others, 7–8
Seven Ordinary Rules for Extraordinary Results, 1–10

Shakespeare, William, 208
simplicity, decisiveness and, 28–9
solutions
    problems and, ix-xii, 222–4
    solutions-orientation and, 95–6
Spielberg, Steven, 85–6
Stachowski, Richie, 159
staking a claim, 131–2
starting over, 116–19
Staubach, Roger, 225
Stewart, James, 165
strengths, recognizing, 63
stress
    managing, 91–6
    problem solvers and, x
    techniques for managing, 94–6
subconsciousness, power of, 77–8, 115
subliminal messages, from others, 78
success
    attitude and, 185–91
    confidence and, 219
    fear of, 118–19
    knowledge and, 87
    necessary for success, 217–24
    planning and, 34
Sutter, Johan, 129–31

talents
    acting on, 12–13, 15
    unacknowledged, 145–6
    See also potential.
talk, power of, 196–7
Templeton, Sir John, 109–10
Thomas, Dave, 135
thoughts
    becoming conscious of, 63
    controlling, 92, 96
    power of, 78–9, 81, 197, 210
    self-defeating, 85
time management, 94, 99–100
toxic relationships, 220
traditions vs. truth, 125
Trump, Donald, 174
turning points, 47–8

unconscious, behavior and, 8–9
"unlearning," 58
"upgrading" life, 211–15

verbal commitments, action vs., 31–6
vision, problem solving and, x, 223

waiting, acting vs., 107–11
Walker, A'Lelia, ix
Walker, Charles Joseph, viii
Walker, Madame C.J. (Sarah Breedlove), vii–ix
wealth building

as intentional act, 11–12
belief and, 64
drive for, 139–40
giving and, 109–10
investing and, 140
See also money.
Winfrey, Oprah, 103, 109
Winters, Jonathan, 108
Woods, Tiger, 161, 174

wisdom
　knowledge and, 104–5, 217, 221
　leadership and, 220
　necessary for success, 217–24
wishes vs. goals, 121

"you," power of word, 164. *See also* individuals, unique value of.

www.ingramcontent.com/pod-product-compliance
Lightning Source LLC
Chambersburg PA
CBHW071605080526
44588CB00010B/1030